Reading in Junior Classes

Reading in Junior Classes

with guidelines to
the revised *Ready to Read* series

Ministry of Education

Learning Media Wellington

Published for the Ministry of Education by
Learning Media Ltd, Box 3293, Wellington, New Zealand.

Fourth impression 1994

Distributed in the United States of America by
Richard C. Owen Publishers Inc., Box 585, Katonah, NY 10536.
Distributed in Australia by
Troll Books of Australia, Box 522, Roseville, New South Wales 2069.

Dewey number 372.4
ISBN 0 477 04090 X
Item number 04090

Contents

Foreword

The publication of this handbook completes the revision of the *Ready to Read* series, first published in 1963. The handbook to the original series, *Suggestions for Teaching Reading in Infant Classes*, written by the late Myrtle Simpson, discussed the principles underlying the teaching of reading to young children. This handbook, *Reading in Junior Classes*, incorporates those ideas and adds knowledge gained from the experience of practising teachers over the past twenty years.

The handbook offers guidance to teachers on the use of the books in the revised and extended *Ready to Read* series, and describes the evolving New Zealand style for teaching reading in the early years. It also discusses the characteristics of skilled readers and teaching approaches which enable children to learn to read.

Many people have had a hand in the writing of this handbook—far too many to acknowledge individually. I take this opportunity, however, to thank those who have been most closely associated with the *Ready to Read* revision—Margaret Mooney, the Editor of *Ready to Read* during the past five years, Joyce Burnett and Pam Coote, who were the co-ordinators of the project at different times, and Doug Helm, Education Officer, Reading.

W. L. Renwick
Director-General of Education

Introduction

Teaching reading in junior classes in New Zealand is based on these beliefs:

Reading programmes should be child centred.

Reading for meaning is paramount.

Reading must always be rewarding.

Children learn to read by reading.

Children learn best on books that have meaning and are rewarding.

The best approach to teaching reading is a combination of approaches.

The best cure for reading failure is good first teaching.

The foundations of literacy are laid in the early years.

The new *Ready to Read* series is designed in keeping with these beliefs.

1 Talking and Reading

The World of Talk and Writing

Babies grow in a world of talk. They hear adults talking to each other, about them, to them. They hear talk on the radio, on TV, in the street, at the shops. From what they hear as growing children, they figure out a crucial understanding about talk: groups of sounds have ideas behind them and are grounded in experience.

The world of babies is also a literate world. Written words crowd in on every side—from the lettered cartons holding their toys, the TV advertisements, the magazines and books at home, to the bright rows of tins and packets on the supermarket shelf, and the flashing lights of neon signs. Later, children will reach the same understanding about written forms as they did about talk: these symbols stand for talk; they express meaning, and relate to the rhymes and jingles, songs and stories that were told them in their early lives.

Babies grow in a world of talk and writing.

But before babies can make something of the language that surrounds them, they must make something of what language is part of and about—the world around.

Making Sense of Experience

The first stages of language growth are rooted in babies' efforts to make experience work for them—especially to grasp and convey meanings.

11

They must "learn how to mean".* Early on, they begin to perceive experience as more than a featureless stream. Events emerge because they are seen to recur in regular or significant ways. Each baby interprets situations with a unique mix of associations, and their individual structuring of experience greatly influences what they make of the language associated with it. Tod, always prevented by his mother from touching anything hot, cried out tearfully, when his sister refused to let him play with her Teddy, "Hot! Hot!"

As they grow, babies begin to turn their understandings into chunks of talk. This early talk does duty in a variety of uses: "Dada car" can mean, "That's Daddy's car", "Daddy's in the car", or "I want to go with Daddy in the car", according to context, the subtleties of grammatical form and structure following rather than preceding attempts to communicate meaning.

Making sense of experience is a continuing process. Many happenings confirm and build up each individual's picture of the world. When new events don't fall easily into place, the old world picture is reorganised to accommodate new insights.

Language is one of the driving forces in making sense of experience, and the rewards of achievement are great. "Eagerness and enthusiasm to talk do not originate in a mere desire for learning or using names; they mark the desire for the detection and conquest of an objective world."**

Later, success in reading will enable the child to conquer other worlds: ". . . more lives than one, more memories than we could ever have from what happened to us: in fact, a whole alternative existence, in our own culture or that of others".†

The structuring of experience is unique to cultures and individuals.

Language plays a vital part in making sense of experience.

Reading extends knowledge and experience.

Learning in Wholes

Experience is understood in wholes, the parts of which may not, at first, be seen as distinct or classifiable. "Car" refers to one car and all vehicles at the same time. When a baby cries with hunger, hunger is the entire world, and the listening parent understands without further explanation. "Up!" calls baby Peter, and his mother will pick him up, or pick up something for him, or look up as context dictates. She will often fill out the words for him, "Yes, Pussy's gone up the tree", responding to what

---

*Michael Halliday in *Learning How to Mean: Explorations in the Development of Language*. Edward Arnold, 1975.
**Ernst Cassirer in *An Essay on Man*. Yale University Press, 1944, pp. 132–3.
†Margaret Meek in *Learning to Read*. The Bodley Head, 1982, p. 21.

he says in total, taking the situation, his tone and gestures, as part of the meaning.

Children learning to read effectively grasp meaning in the same way. They will do best if their approach is not fragmented by learning skills in isolation, words out of context, structure patterns unattached to meanings. Even if some of their reading skills are rudimentary, attempting to use them together, as a skilled reader does, will bring them closest to a full understanding.

Children learn best from whole to part, and not vice versa.

Approximations and Risks

Learning to talk is a formidable task, but babies set about it with the characteristic vigour of natural learners. It is an enormously busy time— the livelong day is spent in eager practice of all manner of skills quite apart from those that make up the complexities of language. The child must be doing. Early listening is practice as active as crying, cooing, babbling, and the first attempts at words; just as, later on, looking precedes overt attempts to understand print.

Children learn to listen by listening. They learn to talk by talking.

There is an observable sequence in language development. Each advance is consolidated until it is a safe enough launching pad for the next venture. As a feeling for how things turn out grows, so does the confidence to predict. What has worked before can be tried out again in different ways and, if confirmed, become a potent addition to the range of ready talk. As children are not so fettered as adults by notions of correctness, there is no limit to what can be tried: "All gone outside," says the toddler as the door shuts.* "You better not do that, betn't you?" says four-year-old Timothy. Adventurous growth, the educated guess, flourishes when children risk such approximations to adult language, when their attempts are accepted by those who matter, and when adult responses are made initially to the meaning of what is said rather than to inaccuracies of form or detail.

Children are adventurous in their use of language, extending patterns they know to make new ones.

Children learn by making "mistakes".

Risk-taking is a way of learning, but children do not take risks unless they feel self-confident. They need freedom to approximate to adult reading behaviour with encouragement and guidance, and without censure.

The running record on the next page shows a child prepared to take a risk and make an informed guess about an unfamiliar word— "Bremen".

---

*M.D.S. Braine in Roger Brown's *A First Language*. Harvard, 1976, p. 119.

"Come with us," said the donkey.
"We're going to Bremen [Blenheim]
to be musicians.
You can be a singer in our band."

√ = correct response. Incorrect attempts are written above the text.

Play and Narrative

Children spend an enormous part of their lives learning about the world through play. Children also play with language, repeating and experimenting with sounds and patterns for the sheer fun of saying the words themselves and, as they play, their talk develops in a characteristic way. They make running commentaries on what they are doing, expounding and explaining to themselves. As Margaret Meek says:

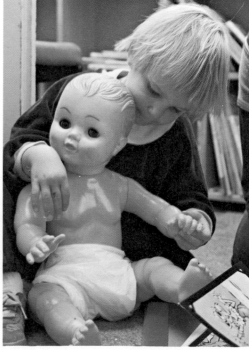

The child talks to his toys about past events and goes over what has happened in different ways of explaining and telling:

"This is my house,
This my mummy house, my daddy house, my Billy house, my granny house,
Houses, houses, houses, his houses,
And mummy goes to work and Billy . . ."

For all that it seems inconsequential, this early talk is by no means random. It performs many functions in children's language learning, but its relevance here is that it is story-telling, the beginning of knowing how to *narrate*.[*]

Play, talk, and make-believe are interwoven, and the boundaries between them stay fluid for a long while, but stories narrated or invented by the child are a kind of play with language, separate from speech, and an essential link between learning to talk and learning to read. Story-telling, whether a child's retelling of past events or of stories told by an adult, is therefore of paramount importance.

Book Language and Book Behaviour

Children learn that language can do many things—get things done, control or interact with others, ask for reasons, show emotion, permit make-believe, define oneself, describe events. They also learn that there are many different ways to talk. They may say, "I want that" to a brother, but, "Please may I have that?" to a teacher. Language varies according to the occasion, to who one is, what one is talking about, and who one is talking to.

As children meet the many different varieties of language, they come across the language of books. Whereas spoken language "takes much of its meaning from the real situation in which it occurs . . . written language . . . must carry the *total* load of meaning without ambiguity. This is the main reason why [it] is more formal, more complete, and more textured than spoken language, and . . . has distinctive structures . . ."[**] Sometimes children confuse book talk and everyday talk. Harriet replied to an invitation to drink some milk with: " 'No', she said, peeping up."

As stories are read to them again and again, children begin to get a feeling for book language. They discover, too, how stories in their own culture are structured—what sort of beginnings, middles, and endings they have. And they discover the special way of reading stories aloud that relates to the chants and nursery rhymes of early childhood.

Story-telling is of paramount importance.

As stories are read to them, children learn about other worlds, book language, story structure, and the "tune" of reading.

---

[*] Margaret Meek in *Learning to Read*. The Bodley Head, 1982. p. 33.
[**] Don Holdaway in *The Foundations of Literacy*. Ashton Scholastic, 1979, p. 54.

". . . when they sit on an adult's knee to listen to a story from a book, they discover that books have their own language, the language of writing. . . . Children meet it in the special tone that accompanies read-ing and stories. For some time they may wonder where it comes from. Then they discover that whoever is reading to them makes the book talk. When, later on, they play at reading, they take up the tune of the story even before they can read the words."*

When young children play at reading, they rehearse the special things a reader does, turning the pages, inspecting the pictures, working over the tune of the words, pausing to savour or to return to particular moments. This is the foundation of successful reading behaviour.

Playing at being a reader is a way of becoming one.

Talking Over Books with Others

Talk serves many purposes. The first, and most obvious for children, is to make and keep contact with the people about them. It is a social use of language. A parent and child, talking over a loved picture book, are talking, as often as not, about themselves in relation to the story, and to each other, as much as about the straight unfolding of the plot. In talking the story through and sharing responses, children come to a fuller understanding of themselves, the story, and of others.

Talking a story over helps readers to understand it and themselves better.

*Margaret Meek in *Learning to Read*. The Bodley Head, 1982, p. 32.

Reaching for Another Point of View

All of us, including small children, sometimes find it hard to understand someone else's point of view (including an author's). In a family of three boys, a child may say that *he* has two brothers, but that each of his brothers has only one, being unable to see himself in another perspective. Yet we often ask young children to empathise by putting themselves in someone else's shoes, or to use their powers of reasoning by drawing some inference which will explain a puzzling situation. An adult may ask, without realising that it may not be an easy question, "How do you think Maui felt when he came back with the tohunga and saw that his brothers had already cut up his fish?" Or, "How could Jack have *seen* the table-top in the giant's castle?"

Entering into the feelings of others is an important part of learning about the emotional power of language, just as the ability to explain logically shows a grasp of rational thought. Asking children how the characters in a story book are feeling, or what the author was trying to convey, encourages the growth of empathy. Explaining a seeming ambiguity, or investigating an aspect systematically, develops observation and the ability to use logical reasoning.

All these are important functions of language in both its spoken and written forms. In extending them, teachers capitalise on children's ability to infer—not only to read the lines but to read between the lines.

Language, Thought, and Symbols

Language is not used only for social purposes. We do not always talk things over with others. But we often use language to find out what we think, and most often, as adults, we do our puzzling silently. Speech has gone inside our heads and become verbal thought.

Thinking includes thinking about language itself. An important understanding about language occurs in a child's dawning speculation about the nature of words themselves. Children realise that words and the things they stand for can be separated, that language can be talked about as well as talked with. They grasp, although not in any conscious, analytical way, that language is a symbolic system.

What children bring to their understanding of these symbols, from within themselves and their own culture, affects their behaviour greatly. People from different cultures may believe that they share the meanings they give to words and actions, while these meanings actually differ. Such people often don't realise this and are trapped in misunderstand-

Stories help children to empathise and to reason.

Language is a symbolic system.

We can fail to reach another viewpoint if we talk past, and not to, each other.

17

ings—" 'talking past each other' . . . unless someone opens their eyes to what is happening . . ."[*]

For most peoples of the world, the relationships between things, ideas, situations, and the verbal or nonverbal symbols that represent them vary enormously. There is no one symbolic system. The meanings attached to body language—eye contact, for example—vary according to culture and situation. For a bicultural child, there can often be a mystifying clash. Seven-year-old Tolovai commented: "It's funny at school, eh? The teacher says it's wrong to stare and then she tells me off for not looking at her." (See pages 66–9 for further comment on children learning English as a second language.)

The meanings each culture attaches to language symbols vary greatly.

Words as Separate Items

In time, young children also begin to realise consciously something they have long made use of—that words are separate items. At first, a baby hears speech as an unbroken flow of sounds. This must be split into meaningful parts before it can be used. Children make what they see as the most significant divisions in the flow of speech first, picking out stressed syllables before weak ones. Mothers instinctively help their babies in this by using emphatic phrasing when they talk to them. Gradually, the child's working analysis is refined, but some distinctions may not come until children meet the written word. " 'Smorning,' write 'smorning' for me," asks five-year-old Susie.

In learning to read, children come to make a one-to-one connection between spoken and written words.

As they begin to read—and for some as they produce their own forms of writing—many children discover that the marks on paper stand for separate words, that these words are the same words they have heard in stories, learnt to say in the flow of speech, and that this written speech also relates to their own experience.

Reading involves relating written words, and the ideas, feelings, and episodes they represent, to background experience.

Teacher: . . . find the page that tells you what Old Tuatara said.
Child: (excitedly pointing to the word "old") Old! Old!
Teacher: Yes, it is. See if you can find it somewhere else.
Child: (turning pages) *It's* got old! . . . Old again! . . . *Again!*

---

[*]Joan Metge and Patricia Kinloch in *Talking Past Each Other*. Victoria University Press, 1978, p. 9.

A Good Start at Home

Lucky children are those whose early life has been rich in language of many kinds. The articulate ones are those who have been played with, sung to, read to, talked with, listened to, with fun, care, and patience.

The good readers are those who have found books and print as much a part of life as kisses and cuddles. These children have had many of their reading skills "handed to them on a golden platter".*

> Harriet and Nana were chatting together as they laid the table. Three-year-old Harriet put the cutlery down carefully and crookedly. "There's a fork for Hattie and a—oh! I can't say 'poon' yet," she beamed, "so I just say 'poon'."
> "That's clever," said Nana. "Can I have a spoon, too?"
> "Poor little Nana," said Harriet. "I forgetted Nana's poon."

This conversation shows two people at home, talking and sharing. The child is taking risks, and making approximations and creative innovations. She is actually on the verge of solving the point at issue, but her self-confidence reflects more than this—it demonstrates a warm, accepting relationship between herself and a guiding adult.

---

*Dorothy Butler in *Babies Need Books*. Penguin, 1982, p. 25.

Continuing Language Growth at School

When children go to school, they have a growing realisation of the meanings and patterns of experience, and of the language that is a significant way of handling that experience. Their language includes a comprehensive and developing control of grammatical structure, a fluent use of sound patterns, and many thousands of items of vocabulary. They know what functions language can fulfil for them and much about its varieties. Their language growth is not complete, but it has developed so far because there have been several important things to foster it. It will continue to grow at school if:

When children start school, they have considerable control over oral language.

- Caring adults share experiences.
- Self-esteem comes from being valued for what they are.
- A host of different models are there for them to imitate.
- Timely guidance draws the most out of even a simple happening.
- They have a wide range of play experiences and the stimulus of a rich environment.
- There is freedom to advance through stages of development in their own time, and to take responsibility for their own progress.
- Others accept the imperfect attempts through which they learn, but show clearly that they expect them to succeed.

Several factors are involved in language growth at school.

Under these conditions,* children come to believe that the complexities of written language can be unravelled, and that the knack of how to do it is not beyond their power.

---

*See Brian Cambourne, "Language, Learning and Literacy", in *Towards a Reading-Writing Classroom* by Andrea Butler and Jan Turbill, Primary English Teaching Association, 1984, chapter 2; and Don Holdaway in *Stability and Change in Literacy Learning*, Heinemann Educational Books, 1984, chapter 2, for conditions under which children learn to speak and to read.

2
The Reading Process

Introduction

What are you doing as you read this? Are you looking carefully at all the letters, joining them into words which make sense? Or are you merely sampling the print, anticipating what comes next, and then doing some rapid checking to make sure that the meaning is what you expected? One thing is certain: you are reading to come to an understanding of the ideas behind the marks on the paper.

When we read, we reconstruct meaning from print. The reading process is the means by which we do it.

The reading process involves reconstructing meaning from print.

Look again at another passage and try to think of what you're doing as you read.

> Unfortunately, he sees the toothbrushes.
> This crocodile loves toothbrushes.
> At home he has forty-two toothbrushes
> all colours,
> but now he wants a new one—a red-striped one.
> Of course I get him a red-striped one,
> otherwise he will make a terrible fuss,
> snapping his jaws and rocking the trolley.
> When you go shopping with a crocodile,
> you have to be understanding.
> That makes forty-three toothbrushes he's got.
> We'll have to start another toothbrush rack.*

You are a skilled reader. You didn't read every word. You sampled or selected some parts of the text and, drawing on experience, you built up expectations of the passage which were refined and extended as you became familiar with its intent, mood, and style. These expectations became predictions, which you confirmed by sampling the text further, but only to the least extent necessary to establish meaning. It is only when meaning is lost that a reader has to attend more closely to the print, perhaps rereading or reading on, and looking to other sources of information.

Skilled readers sample text rather than focusing on every detail.

*Margaret Mahy in *Shopping with a Crocodile*. *Ready to Read* series. Department of Education, 1983, p. 8.

There's more. Skilled readers don't use only the information available from the print—they *bring* vital information to any act of reading from their knowledge of language and of the world. *Reading is an interaction between what is on the page and what is in the reader's head.*

Reading is an interactive process.

Skilled reading, therefore, is not a process of identifying all the letters, and linking these to make words which in turn make sentences conveying meaning. As Marie Clay says, "We should only dwell on detail long enough for the child to discover its existence and then encourage the use of it in isolation only when absolutely necessary."* A skilled reader is concerned with meaning first and uses it to determine how much attention needs to be given to the print in confirming or correcting predictions, and also in predicting further. Look at this passage and notice how much you depend on this way of reading.

The more readers understand, the less they need to read every word.

When I _____ to _____ shops,
I always have to t_____ my croc_____ with _____ .
He _____ pleased to g_____ for a walk.
He waves his t_____ _____ smile _____ at every _____ .
Not _____y p_____ple s_____ b_____ck.
They j_____ blink and _____ are.**

Did you have to pause anywhere for extra thought? What "threw" you? How did you overcome this difficulty? Did you attend to meaning first, or to syntax? Did you notice that you, as a skilled reader, have learned how to reduce to a minimum the attention you give to print details, and so are able to read quickly and efficiently? Margaret Meek puts it like this:

Skilled readers attend to meaning and syntax before print details.

> As [the reader] brings the text to life, he casts back and forth in his head for connections between what he is reading and what he already knows. His eyes scan forward or jump backwards. He pauses, rushes on, selects from his memory whatever relates the meaning to his experience or his earlier reading, in a rich and complex system of to-ing and fro-ing in his head, storing, reworking, understanding or being puzzled.†

Cues from Meaning, Structure, Sound, and Print

The information used by a reader to reconstruct meaning comes from several sources which are known as cues. They are:

- *Semantic cues*, from the *meanings* which have become associated with language through experience. (If there has been no experience, a verbal symbol is just a sound, or a mark on paper. Meanings differ according

Semantic cues.

---

*Marie Clay in *The Early Detection of Reading Difficulties*. Heinemann Educational Books, 3rd ed., 1985, p. 13.
**Margaret Mahy in *Shopping with a Crocodile*. *Ready to Read* series. Department of Education, 1983, p. 2.
†Margaret Meek in *Learning to Read*. The Bodley Head, 1982, p. 21.

to experience: if you live in the USA, "freezing workers" are people who are very cold. In New Zealand, they are employees in the meat industry.)

- *Syntactic cues*, based on familiarity with the *structure* of written language, i.e., how words are organised into patterns. (Compare "the blind Venetian" and "the Venetian blind", or "they made him King" with "they made him a jacket".)

  Syntactic cues.

- *Grapho-phonic cues*,* which enable the reader to identify individual letters, or patterns of letters, in clusters, affixes, roots, and whole words, either instantly at sight or from their associated *sounds*. (Compare, for example, "right/write" and "bad/bed".)

  Grapho-phonic cues.

- *The conventions of print*: directionality, the use of punctuation, spaces, capital and lower case letters to show (mainly) where a sentence, a word, or a paragraph begins and ends. (Compare, "On the picnic, we had ham, sandwiches, fruit, salad, and lemonade" with, "On the picnic, we had ham sandwiches, fruit salad, and lemonade".)

  The conventions of print.

The following running record shows a child using semantic cues throughout, syntactic cues to produce a verb at "woke up", graphophonic cues at "felt", and print conventions to return to the beginning of the second sentence because meaning has been lost.

✓ ✓ ✓ ✓ walked sc ✓
At last the wolf woke up.
✓ ✓ f-f-fighted ✓)sc
He felt terrible! Child: "And a good job, too!"

SC = self-corrects. The arrow indicates the point to which the child returned in rerunning the text. The child's and the teacher's comments are written beside the text.

Strategies—Making Use of Cues

Cues are sources of information. Strategies are the ways the reader makes use of cues.

Sampling a text comes first.

Reading may be thought of as a constantly repeated process of *sampling*, *predicting*, *confirming*, and *self-correcting*. At the outset, the text is sampled, and significant visual features are searched for and picked out, some words and/or letters being instantly recognised.

On this basis, predictions of meaning and text are made. This enlightened guessing makes use of the reader's background experience and

On the basis of sampling, predictions are made.

*Some authorities refer to these cues as "visual information".

oral language, and the semantic, syntactic, and grapho-phonic cues which the sampling has brought into focus.

Further sampling may confirm the predictions and the flow of meaning may be established. If predictions are not confirmed, further searching is done to aid self-correction by rereading, reading on, or referring to other cues.

Predictions are confirmed or corrected by further sampling.

Sampling, predicting, confirming, and self-correcting are the strategies through which the act of reading takes place. These strategies constantly interact with and support each other. In experienced readers, the process seems to be largely automatic.

It is the ability to use these strategies quickly, confidently, and independently, which activates what Marie Clay calls a reader's "self-improving system". She says:

Using strategies successfully and independently makes up a self-improving system.

> The end-point of *early* instruction has been reached when children have a self-improving system, which means that they learn more about reading every time they read, independent of instruction. . . . they engage in "reading work", a deliberate effort to solve new problems with familiar information and procedures. They notice new things about words . . . The newly-noticed feature(s) of print, worked upon today, becomes the reference point for another encounter in a few days.*

Children are learning how to learn when they are helped to work actively on the problems they meet in new text and find solutions for themselves. They come to rely on their own problem-solving abilities, and to think independently. Independent problem-solving on increasingly difficult books enables children to contribute to their own learning. It helps them to teach themselves. The strategies, and how children acquire them, will be discussed more fully in chapter 3.

*Marie Clay in *The Early Detection of Reading Difficulties*. Heinemann Educational Books, 3rd. ed., 1985, p. 14.

The following running record shows a child who has developed and is making use of a self-improving system.

> ✓ ✓ ✓ pup
> She met a puppy.
> ✓ ✓ ✓ ✓
> "Where are you going
> ✓ ✓ ✓
> on your tricycle?"
> ✓ ✓ pup sc
> barked the puppy.

Child: "Is that pup, or puppy?"
Teacher: "What do you think?"
Child: "Puppy. Then the other one should be puppy, too."
Teacher: "How can you be sure?"
Child: "There's more letters"

Understandings About Reading

Skilled readers have acquired some important understandings about books, written text, and the reading process.

Books
- Books, like spoken language, have the power to delight or dismay, to enlighten or confuse, to challenge, and to satisfy.
- They provide the answers to almost any question, and assist greatly in understanding oneself and the world.

Written Text
- Written text is a representation of spoken language and will almost certainly make sense.
- The conventions of print and books are consistent.

The Reading Process
- Meaning is won by integrating information from several cues.
- Not every letter or every word has to be processed every time in reconstructing meaning.
- Risk-taking is not only desirable but essential for efficient reading.
- Self-improvement in reading is achieved by using strategies flexibly and independently.

The Right Attitudes

Skilled readers have also developed positive attitudes to reading.
- They are interested in ideas and books, seeing them as relevant to their daily lives and their deepest personal concerns.
- They insist on making sense of what they read.
- They have confidence in their self-improving system and attribute their success to it.

The following running record shows an interested child reacting to a satisfying end to a story.

The stones inside him
were very heavy.
They dragged him
into the water, *sc*
and he sank *sunk* to the bottom
for ever. *of sc*

Child: "Good – 'cause he
went to the bottom."

— = The child omits the word.

3
Developing the Strategies

The Teacher's Role

It makes sense to have children behaving like skilled readers to the fullest extent possible from the beginning, and it is the teacher's role to help children develop the strategies, understandings, and attitudes outlined in chapter 2. Here are some important basic considerations.

Just as parents and caring adults encourage children to acquire spoken language by taking risks, teachers should encourage children to take risks in their reading. Teachers should think of "mistakes" as "miscues"* and, by accepting children's approximations, assist them in learning the techniques of confirmation and self-correction as aspects of self-improvement in reading. As the children gain the skill and confidence to regulate their own reading, they understand that taking risks and making miscues are a natural part of the reading process.

Sampling, predicting, confirming, and self-correcting so that the message is understood are familiar to children from their experience of acquiring spoken language. However, it is important for teachers to see that unrecognised words are in children's spoken or listening vocabulary before expecting them to apply the above strategies effectively in beginning reading.

Teachers can develop children's ability to sample, predict, confirm, and self-correct while reading by drawing their attention to appropriate cues. This should be done in ways which children themselves will make growing use of as they develop into independent readers. Skilful questioning and allowing plenty of time for children to work things out are essential.

Teachers should see that they don't rob children of the opportunity to learn for themselves by saying, "That's right" or, "That's wrong" but rather, "Well, does that seem right?" and, "How can you be sure?" Teachers also need to reinforce independent behaviour by saying such things as, "I'm pleased you thought that out all by yourself". This parallels the way parents have encouraged their children when they were learning to talk.

Sensitive observation of what a child *actually does while reading* provides a teacher with information about what the child has understood, what attitudes prevail, and what the child needs to learn next. This observation should also extend to what the child brings to reading in the way of pre-school experience and language ability.

The teacher's role is to help children develop good reading behaviour.

Approximations are a way of learning.

Predicting and confirming are familiar strategies.

Questioning techniques are important.

Children need the chance to accept responsibility for their own learning.

Sensitive observation is essential.

---

*"Miscue" is a term first used by Kenneth Goodman. It refers to an approximation through which a reader works towards meaning.

31

At school entry, children normally have a fairly full knowledge of language and many experiences to draw on, but have to learn more about the special language of books, grapho-phonic cues, and the conventions of print. The former is best acquired by reading widely. The latter cues and conventions will be acquired most successfully if teachers highlight them in the course of rewarding reading done within a balanced programme, and in combination with the cues which children can already use.

Learning about cues should be done in the course of rewarding reading.

Children, learning to read, have to pay particular attention to print. It is sometimes necessary, then, to have them focus on detail. They may temporarily isolate, for example, a letter, and identify the sound usually associated with it. But any learning of separate items needs to be combined with other items of information, both in the text and within the reader, before its use is truly understood and applied. Separate items of learning need to be *taken back into reading*, i.e., teachers should ensure that any item which has been isolated for attention should be looked at again in its original context, and what has been learned applied later in other contexts.

Teachers need to take back into reading those items temporarily isolated for closer attention.

The essential strategies, understandings, and attitudes are learned best as children read texts which have special meaning for them, which use their natural language, are not too difficult, and which they take a delight in reading. Books in the *Ready to Read* series have been produced specifically to meet these requirements. Many of the other books essential to support *Ready to Read* are listed in *Books for Junior Classes* (see page 97).

Texts should have intrinsic value.

Learning How to Sample

Helping beginning readers to sample effectively means showing them how to attend only to those details of meaning and print which are necessary to make predictions and to confirm or correct them. Making sampling effective depends largely on helping children make use of:
- Sight vocabulary (words they have learned to recognise on sight).
- Significant details of print.

An effective sample is never bigger than it has to be.

Sampling Using Sight Vocabulary

Skilled readers sample effectively because they know a great number of words at sight, and the phrases and patterns they frequently occur in. For children, this knowledge cannot be aquired overnight; it comes as a result of four main types of activity:

- Extensive reading of the many kinds of text used in a rich and balanced reading programme.
- Language experience which makes many spoken words familiar in their written forms.
- Children's own writing, where they use some common words and phrases over and over again.
- Seeing the same words and phrases in many contexts, in notices, on labels and signs, on television, etc., in the classroom and outside.

Building a sight vocabulary involves four main types of activity.

Teaching words out of context deprives the child of their meaning.

The significance of acquiring sight vocabulary in these ways is that the words are learned in context. The parent of a young child who was heard to say, "When I was at school, we had the 'words-in-a-tin' method" was reflecting the teacher's belief that, if only children could learn the words, the rest of reading would somehow take care of itself. However, as the Department of Education's handbook on reading points out:

> . . . new words are worked out by using a combination of the context, the intial sound of the words and the spoken language experience of the

reader. Each time such a "new" word appears in the child's reading, it is identified more rapidly until it is recognised immediately and becomes part of the sight vocabulary. This emphasises the need for wide and varied reading at each stage.*

Sampling Using Print Details

Skilled readers also sample effectively because of their extensive knowledge of letters, clusters of letters, affixes, roots, and compound words. Children learning to read acquire this knowledge over time through the kinds of experience described above and particularly through becoming familiar with the form and arrangements of letters as they learn handwriting. Teachers can focus children's attention on particular letter clusters, affixes, etc., in handwriting lessons, and by using techniques such as a masking device during shared reading, or a small teaching blackboard during guided reading.

Children build up a knowledge of print details over time.

From early on, children may begin to select different items which help the reading process—a child who notices a detail in a picture is sampling; a child who has learned the shape of the letter which begins his or her name can scan text and pick out that letter. Most beginning readers, however, attend to virtually everything. The skill of sampling only essential cues comes slowly, and with practice. It follows the stage

Sampling words follows the stage of locating them one by one.

*Reading: Suggestions for Teaching Reading in Primary and Secondary Schools. Department of Education, 1972, p. 74.

of locating words one by one, for example, by finger pointing and "voice pointing".* Reading easy books and rereading familiar texts enables the child to practise the strategy without pressure.

Prediction

From what the reader has sampled of the text, predictions are made. Prediction is based on the expectations created by experience. A reader's semantic, syntactic, and grapho-phonic expectations of a text become more precise and encompassing as the reading progresses and understanding grows. As Marie Clay says, "I define reading as a message-gaining, problem-solving activity, which increases in power and flexibility the more it is practised."**

Prediction is based on the expectations created by experience.

One of the props on which prediction rests is context—the experiences and language surrounding words which fix their meanings. Frank Smith says that the "two best clues to any word are its total *context*—the meaning in which it is embedded—and its similarity [in form] to words that are already known."† Context helps the reader's prediction by narrowing down possibilities. A reader uses semantic context when predicting, for example, from a picture of an empty nest, that the story is about birds or, sampling the word "tiki", predicts the story is about Maoridom.

Context helps to establish meaning by reducing unlikely alternatives.

Readers also make use of syntactic context, or grapho-phonic context. They know that some words associate with one grammatical form rather than another (e.g., "several books" not "several book"), that certain letters regularly appear with others (e.g., th, ng) and in particular positions in words.

Teachers often capitalise on the way context helps prediction by "the prior elimination of unlikely alternatives".†† For example, in reference to meaning they may say, "Look at the picture on the cover. Look at the title. What do you think this story is going to be about?" Teachers make use of children's knowledge of the syntactic patterns of their language in a similar way by asking, "What word could make sense there?" And they make use of the child's grapho-phonic knowledge with questions such as, "We often meet that letter/those letters at the beginning of words. Can you think of a word that makes sense and looks right?"

---

*"Voice pointing" is a term use by Marie Clay to describe the way young children, making normal progress, say the text word by word, with breaks between each word (see Marie Clay in *Reading: The Patterning of Complex Behaviour.* 2nd. ed., Heinemann Educational Books, 1979, p. 141).
**Marie Clay (as above) p. 6.
†Frank Smith in *Reading.* Cambridge University Press, 1978, p. 67.
††Frank Smith (as above) p. 85.

Predictions in reading make most use of two kinds of cues: the semantic—concerned largely with meaning (what is likely to happen)—and the syntactic—concerned largely with form (what grammatical structure is likely to come next in the text). Look at these sentences and notice what use you make of context to predict the meaning and the grammatical form of the missing words. This is similar to what we do with words we find hard to read and is an example of the "cloze" procedure.

He took off his hat and coat and sat _____.

After dinner, we washed the _____.

He shouted _____, "Stop thief!"

We predict both the events that are going to happen and the language that will represent them.

Providing for Prediction

Because semantic and syntactic predictions are important parts of the reading process, they can be encouraged by selecting material at the right level of difficulty, and making sure that most of the concepts and vocabulary come within the children's experience. If this experience is lacking, the teacher should ensure that it is gained before reading by making visits, showing pictures or objects, and discussing in context the new vocabulary and concepts, or words used in unfamiliar ways. As Don Holdaway says:

> The most highly predictable material is something which [the child's] brain produced before—hence the power of language experience techniques by which children read what they themselves have written.* (see page 65)

Once the teacher is sure that the children have sufficient experience and that the level of difficulty is suitable, the next step is to set a clear purpose for reading by having the children think ahead about a story in response to questions.

Setting a clear purpose for reading aids prediction.

Using Predictions in the Reading Lesson

It is useful during the first reading of a new story, in shared and guided reading, to have the children predict the next word on several occasions.

Where appropriate during reading, to aid prediction, help children make use of their knowledge of the many syntactic relationships between words, e.g., that the gender of personal pronouns relates them to particular nouns ("*That crocodile* loves toothbrushes. At home *he* has forty-two . . ."); that, out of a choice of possible nouns, the definite article often points to the particularised thing ("the *biggest cake in the world*"); that singular and plural nouns, determiners, and verbs agree with each other ("*these* boots *are . . . , this* boot *is . . .*").

---

*Don Holdaway in *Stability and Change in Literacy Learning.* Heinemann Educational Books, 1984, p. 17.

Teachers can also use oral and written cloze examples to help children discover the power of semantic and syntactic cues.

The following running record shows a child leaving out an unknown word and using the rest of the sentence, together with what has gone before, to predict, supply, and confirm a difficult word.

"My master wanted to cook me
for dinner, so I ran away,"
said the rooster.   Child: "Oh! Dinner!"

Another running record shows a child sampling and predicting (intelligently but incorrectly) "several", and later returning and self-correcting. Note that only a *plural* determiner, "several", was considered possible before a plural noun, "kids". Here the child was using a knowledge of syntactic, as well as grapho-phonic, cues.

The Wolf and the Seven Little Kids

retold by **Fran Hunia**

pictures by **Nina Price**

Child "And that's like seven goats!"

Once there was a mother goat
who had seven little kids.   s-several
One day, she called to her kids.   calls
"I have to go out
to look for food," she said.
"Do not open the door   Don't sc
while I'm away,   When
or the wolf will come in   comes sc
and eat you up."

"How shall we know the wolf   sh-   sc
if he comes?"
asked the seven little kids.   asks sc   Child: "Oh, now I know. That's seven."

37

Confirmation and Self-Correction

As soon as a prediction is made, the reader looks for confirmation. The minimum amount of information necessary is rapidly selected from the available cues, and cross-checked. Where there is uncertainty, and self-correction is needed, additional cues may be brought into play. For example, when meaning is lost, a reader may look at other significant letters in a word to identify a root or ending, or check on the conventions of print. This further search is always regulated by what makes sense, and confirmed by rereading or reading on.

The following running record shows a child reading over a full-stop and losing meaning. After reading "window", the child paused, realising that the text did not make sense, and corrected the mistake.

The ghost comes to an old house.
By the window. |sc
is an old, old woman.

⊙ = Full-stop omitted;   . = full-stop inserted.
                          ∧

The teacher can help children learn to confirm predictions by ensuring that:

- The text is not so difficult in concepts and language that children have to self-correct too often—often at the expense of meaning.
- Children are made responsible for confirming and correcting their own predictions by answering questions such as, "Does that make sense?" or, "How do you know?".
- Children use their knowledge of the available cues, and learn to combine these in various ways as they work at reconstructing meaning.

Too many difficulties may rob a reader of powerful semantic and syntactic cues.

Integrating the Strategies

Successful readers use and integrate the full range of strategies. A child with few strategies may misuse them habitually and fail repeatedly. Such children may come to rely on memory, on sounding words out, or on the assistance of others. Teachers need to identify what a child can do,

Using too few strategies can form unproductive reading habits.

and help each one build up new strategies so that they learn to read better the more they read.

When a teacher is helping children to integrate the strategies in this way, it is important to see that:

- Children are given time to work things out for themselves, and are encouraged when they show independence.
- Children, even when using grapho-phonic cues to analyse a word, or to attend to special features of print, realise that they are searching for something that makes sense.
- Even if neither rereading nor reading on yields meaning immediately, these techniques are what children should be encouraged to try first. They distract the reader least from reconstructing meaning.

Let us say that a child cannot read the word "fetch" in the *Ready to Read* book, *Paru has a Bath*. The following is typical of the help teachers need to give repeatedly to overcome such difficulties.

First, refer to the illustration and ask an opening question such as, "What do you think Hana would tell Paru to do?" The child might respond with a prediction, using the picture and background experience. The teacher could then encourage the child to correct or confirm this attempt by saying some of these things:

- "Try reading from the beginning again, and think what would fit." (This suggestion is particularly useful for very young children. Here the child is predicting.)

Teachers need to help children integrate strategies.

- "Leave the word out, read on and think about what would make sense. Then come back and see if it fits." (Predicting, using cloze, semantic and syntactic cues.)
- "*Does* that make sense?" (Confirming, using semantic and syntactic cues.)
- "Are you sure?" or, "How do you know for sure?" (Cross-referencing, confirmation, responsibility for self-correction.)
- "What does your word begin with?" (Sampling of grapho-phonic cues—significant letters.) "Is it the same?" (Confirmation by cross-referencing to known items.)
- "Are you happy with that?" (Responsibility for confirmation.)
- "Would you like to read that again?" (Starting over again to do a double check, putting the word back into context, and perhaps self-correcting.)

These are the sorts of questions which children, in time, will learn to ask and answer for themselves, and are at the heart of a self-improving system.*

Being able to ask oneself the right questions is the basis of a self-improving system.

The following running record shows a child asking questions about the text.

Child: "What's that? It should be n—nock. Is it?"

So ✓ ✓ k—
Soon there was a knock at the door.
✓ ✓ calls sc
A voice called,
✓ here sc ✓ ✓ kids
"I'm home, my dear children.
✓ ✓ ✓
Open the door."

---

*Marie Clay outlines the goals of a self-improving system in *The Early Detection of Reading Difficulties*. Heinemann Educational Books, 3rd ed., 1985, p. 74.
   "Teachers aim to produce independent readers whose reading improves whenever they read. In independent readers:
      early strategies are secure and habituated,
      the child *monitors* his own reading,
      he *searches* for cues in word sequences, in meaning, in letter sequences,
      he *discovers* new things for himself,
      he *cross-checks* one source of cues with another,
      he *repeats* as if to *confirm* his reading so far,
      he *self-corrects*, assuming the initiative for making cues match,
      he *solves* new words by these means."

Book Language and its Relation to Oral Language

One of the challenges children face is to grasp the distinctions between oral language and written language, especially the particular structures and vocabulary characteristic of the stories they read. Frank Smith says, "Constructions that are common in children's books, such as *What splendid teeth the beaver has,* or *Down the road hand in hand ran Susie and her friend* seem simple and straightforward to most of us only because of our familiarity with written language; they are not the kind of language anyone of us is likely to be accustomed to from everyday speech."[*]

Children, especially those learning English as a second language, become familiar with book language only through experience. All children need help in sorting out the differing styles of oral and written language.

The following running record shows a child confused by the book language "night fell".

There are many differences between speech and book language.

The donkey, the dog, the cat
and the rooster went on together.
Night *field* fell, and the animals
were cold, hungry and tired.

Learning About Print

In a programme which encourages the use of books from the start, meaning and structure of language will be the dominant sources of cues at first, but gradually children become aware of print. From initially telling or retelling the story in their own words, they begin to see if the text could have said what they expected it to say. They begin to search with their eyes and brains to note details which they can interpret. They are beginning to explore the print, always within the context of meaning. This increased attention to print details occurs during the first year at school.

Reading for meaning, therefore, doesn't mean that children should

An increased attention to print follows the stage of children retelling the story in their own words.

---

*Frank Smith in *Reading*. Cambridge University Press, 1978, p. 144.

dispense with actively learning about grapho-phonic cues and the characteristics of written text. They are a necessary part of learning to read and are best done *in the course of real reading* and writing.*

The following running record shows an emergent reader inventing text in a retelling of the story.

— — — — —
We went up the track,

— — — —
and the rain came down

✓ ✓ ✓ ✓ ✓
We put up the tent,
✓ *it rains* — —
and the rain came down.

Dad's ✓ ✓ ✓
Dad cooked a meal,
✓ *its rained and rained.*
and the rain came down.

Mother said, "No sun,"
"No sun," said Mum.
and Father said, "Bad luck.
"Too bad," said Dad.

Come off — shoes
Off came our boots.
Come off — socks
Off came our socks.

— — — — —
We paddled in the stream...

— — — — —
and the rain came down.

✓
Rain.
✓
Rain.
✓
Rain.

Concepts about Print

Children should be acquiring these concepts about print from the beginning:

Directionality

- What end a book starts at.
- The left-hand page is read before the right-hand page.
- The message starts at the top of a page, moves along the lines from left to right, returns to the left on the next line, goes down the page line by line, and continues at the top of the next page.
- What the first letter or cluster of letters in a word are and how the reader, using grapho-phonic cues, moves from left to right.

Print Conventions and One-to-One Matching

- What constitutes a letter, a word, and a sentence.
- The functions of space in relation to words, line-ends, sentences, paragraphs.
- The significance of small and capital letters.
- The use of punctuation, particularly of the full-stop, the question mark, and speech marks.

Cover and Illustrations

- What the cover and title pages are.
- How the illustrations relate to the text.

Children need to acquire these essential understandings, and teachers should provide many opportunities for this learning to occur. Directionality may be supported, early in beginning reading, by finger pointing, as children match the words they are saying with words in the text. Later, these movements become an efficient mental habit. (Voice pointing is another support at the early stages of learning to read.)

Shared reading, where teachers use enlarged texts with a pointer, is a particularly effective way of highlighting print conventions. Guided silent reading also offers frequent opportunities to check whether print conventions have been understood.

Writing provides regular experience for acquiring the necessary knowledge. Teachers write in front of children. They say the words as they write them down so that children become aware of how print conventions are used. The children's spontaneous writing provides the teacher with evidence of what the child has learned and what help needs to be given next. Language experience techniques demonstrate firstly the use of print conventions in writing down children's language, and later how meaning can be reconstructed, using the same conventions.

Don Holdaway says:

> Helping children to identify and clarify the conventions of print in specific terms is as necessary as helping them to depend on meaning and the larger structures of language to develop efficient self-improving processes. . . . It will support and not supplant the learning system of each learner, and will express itself in respect and trust for the divergent ways in which children teach themselves the tasks they wish to master.*

Teachers need to monitor children's progress to make sure they know the essential concepts about print.

Ways of Learning the Letters of the Alphabet

Margaret Meek writes that "the child who plays at reading by imitating what readers seem to do is in a better position to begin to read than those whose first step is instruction in the alphabet."** No one denies, however, that, at some stage, children need to know about the alphabet. Letter names provide consistent labels for these language symbols and, in most cases, provide some clues for the sounds commonly associated with them.

The learning of letter names is most effective when it is enjoyable and its purpose clear. Teachers should use letter names naturally in the course of reading and writing, and learning handwriting, and show why

Knowledge of letters is essential.

---

*Don Holdaway in *The Foundations of Literacy*. Ashton Scholastic, 1979, p. 202.
**Margaret Meek in *Learning to Read*. The Bodley Head, 1982, p. 22.

a knowledge of the alphabet is useful. Here are some ways to achieve this.

- Build up a large, clear wall frieze of the alphabet, get the children to add examples to it regularly, and show them how to use it.
- See that a variety of attractively illustrated alphabet books and simple dictionaries is available (see page 97 for a reference to the classified guide for teachers, *Books for Junior Classes*), and give guidance on their use.

Children need help in learning letters and using the alphabet.

- Get the children to make their own alphabet books, individually, as a group, or as a class, using children's drawings or magazine cut-outs.
- Provide, and encourage the use of, alphabetically-arranged word files for use in the children's own writing.
- Have shared reading and songs which use alphabet rhymes and games.
- Play alphabet games, such as *I Spy*.
- Use magnetic letters, coloured paper cut-outs of letters, sand-trays, sandpaper and felt letters, tracing paper.

  It is better to take examples from the children's actual reading than to manufacture them. However, in reference to such games and exercises, it is most important to remember that children should not waste time on letter games when they could be reading well-chosen books.

45

Learning about Print through Writing

Writing has a considerable contribution to make in learning to read. It can be claimed that it is an integral part of gaining control over written language. When children are writing a simple story they are involved in a building-up process of putting together letters and words which make up sentences. As well, the left to right conventions are being re-inforced. Handwriting practice helps many children become familiar with the forms of letters; some children will invent their own letter forms and spellings.

Learning to write supports learning to read.

Spelling and Reading

Children who invent spelling are actively trying to master the complex-ities of writing. They make "mistakes" because they want to try out their considered analysis of sounds, words, and symbols. Their self-correction is based on discovery of a better set of rules and a desire to "get it right". They arrive at correct spelling through trial and error in the course of writing down things that matter to them. A teacher who permits children to write freely is giving them the chance to "trust their own ears and their own judgments".*

In inventing spelling, children pass through four overlapping stages:

Children's invented spelling goes through several stages.

• *Pre-communicative*

The earliest expression of a child's hypothesis about how alphabetic symbols represent words. The writing could be a hotchpotch of letters, and/or symbols. e.g.,

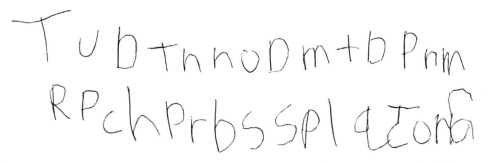

• *Semi-phonetic*

One-, two-, three-letter spellings that show some sound-letter correspondence e.g.,

wnt	—	went
dg	—	dog
B	—	beach

---

*Carol Chomsky in "Write First Read Later", *Childhood Education*, vol. 47 (1971), pp. 296–299.

A child may make use of alphabet names here, e.g.,

- *Phonetic*

  Characterised by an almost perfect match between sounds and letters,
  e.g.,

becos	—	because
wot	—	what
sed		said

  Wen ski was finsd I wnt to

  the Libee my m sed to me haRee up
  and I fwnd sum bks.

- *Transitional*

  A major move towards standard spelling, with less reliance on sounds
  for representing words and a much greater reliance on visual aspects
  of print, e.g.,

huose	—	house
eightee	—	eighty

  sanly is going to tne
  Vet to Day to Hav
  a heeble and He
  is going to sta
  the niet thre
  and sanly climb tee
  and #Bits toes

47

Teachers who are aware of these stages can analyse miscues to determine what the child understands, and to decide what should be taught next. A child's invented spellings could show the degree of knowledge of:
- Alphabet and letter names.
- Letter-sound relationships.
- Directional rules.
- Concepts of a letter or a word.
- The functions of space.
- The ordering of letters within a word.
- The sequence of sounds within a word.
- Punctuation.

Letter-Sound Relationships (Grapho-phonic Cues) in Reading

When children find that they can't recognise a word, or need to confirm one, they often need to attend more closely to letters or letter clusters. A skilled reader identifies these rapidly and links them with sounds to suggest a word that fits the sense of the passage, or predicts the word and checks that its sounds are represented by the letter on the page. It is very seldom that every letter in a word has to be identified and its related sounds blended, because the reader bears in mind and uses the available semantic and syntactic cues.

The English spelling system doesn't always associate one sound with one symbol, but does regularly indicate some grammatical forms. For example, "boxed" and "played", both end in different sounds but are represented by the same symbols "-ed". This cues the reader in to the idea of past tense and is helpful in gaining meaning. The hindrance of English spelling lies in the many inconsistencies in letter-sound relationships. For example, the sounds represented by letters vary—consider the letter "a" in "mask", "easy", "make", "said", "machine", and so on. Using grapho-phonic cues, therefore, as the *first* method of dealing with a problem often interferes with understanding: children may shut off from meaning as they struggle with mechanical difficulties. It is better that children predict meaning from other cues at the outset and use their knowledge of the relationships of letters and sounds for confirmation.

There are both advantages and disadvantages in English spelling.

Helping Children to Discover and Use Letter-Sound Relationships

As described in previous sections, there are many ways in which children, in the early stages of learning to read and write, can be made aware of the names and forms of letters. Children also need plenty of

Listening practice is important.

48

practice in listening, so that they learn to hear similarities and to discriminate between sounds. They must learn to associate sounds correctly with particular letters, or letter clusters. Teachers often begin by drawing children's attention to the sounds related to the first letters of their names.

At a later stage, usually in the context of a guided reading lesson, a letter (or letter cluster) may be isolated for special attention when opportunities lie ahead to apply and confirm the knowledge of its associated sound. Children may be helped to listen and look for similarities and differences in sequences* such as:

Boots, Toots   (*Boots for Toots*)
school, Pool   (*Our Teacher, Miss Pool*)
grew, flew   (*Blackbird's Nest*)
truck, trailer   (*The Biggest Cake in the World*)
four big babies   (*Blackbird's Nest*)
a pot of pepper   (*Greedy Cat*)

The recommended practice is to have children discover the letter-sound relationship, working from the known to the unknown by following the steps of:

Working from the known to the unknown helps children discover letter-sound relationships.

- *Listening*, to identify the sound without seeing the letter(s).
- *Looking and listening*, to identify the written form of the letter and to associate a sound.
- *Applying the new knowledge*, to take it back into reading.

A typical lesson follows this pattern:

Listen to these words. You know them all: ten, top, tiny. Say them slowly after me: ten, top, tiny.

Again: ten, top, tiny.

What do you think is the same about them?

Let's have a look at these words now and let's say them again: ten, top, tiny (pointing left to right on the board or chart).

What do you notice about them? Let's underline the letter that is the same in each word: ten, top, tiny. What is its name? Whose name starts the same way? What other words begin the same way? or, Whose name starts with a "t"? or, What things in the room start with "t"? (These should be written up.) Let's look at these sentences (from Boots for Toots), and see if we can use what we have just learned to work out some missing words:

"These boots are too . . . ." (tall)

"These boots are too . . . ." (tight)

Applying the knowledge by using meaning and syntax to help understand letter-sound relationships.

---

*The sequences are taken from *Ready to Read* books.

49

(Accept all offerings, asking, *Does that make sense?* or, *How can you be sure that's right?*)

It is most important to have children applying what they have learned as a confirmation strategy when they are engaged in reading continuous text. Teachers should note two final points:

- Because it is very difficult to give sounds to consonants in isolation, and because most vowels represent several sounds, it is less confusing for children if letters are called by their letter *names*.
- While letters in the initial position are the *most* useful in identifying words, it is also sometimes necessary to attend to letters in the final position, or even in the medial one.

The lesson outlined above is easily adapted to present: consonant clusters such as, sh-, ch-, tr-, str-; long and short vowel sounds, and/or vowel blends; prefixes and suffixes such as, un-, re-, -er, -ly.

Compound Words, Root Words, and Contractions

It is best to work on these forms as they occur in reading texts. For example, it is more in keeping with real reading to have children use the context of a story to help analyse "milkman" into its components than to complete an exercise joining "milk" and "man", and other pairs of words.

Working from whole to part in analysing compound words is more in keeping with real reading.

Syllabification

Syllabification can be a useful aid in identifying a word, but it is seldom necessary for a skilled reader to syllabify a word completely. Skilled readers usually find that recognising the first syllable of a word in context is enough to identify it. It is recommended that teaching children the rudiments of syllabification be kept until they are nearing the end of the *Ready to Read* series. Detailed guidance is available in the handbook, *Reading: Suggestions for Teaching Reading in Primary and Secondary Schools,* Department of Education, 1972, pages 95–103.

Teaching syllabification is not a pre-requisite for reading.

Finally, as Brian Cambourne points out, diversity in learning to read reflects the diversity of human nature:

> . . . there were no neat and clean stages. Each child created and solved his or her own problems, and this was how he or she learned, moving inexorably, but by different routes, to the same destination.*

---

*Brian Cambourne, "Learning about Learning", in *English in Australia*, no. 66, December 1983, p. 25.

4
A Balanced Reading Programme

The Importance of Attitude

Children are well on the way to reading if they have had a good start in language, and rewarding early reading experiences. Children from stimulating and loving homes become confident and articulate speakers. When they go to school, a rich developmental programme and a caring teacher enable them to go on learning naturally. Such a programme fosters good attitudes to learning and to others. If these are in place, the rest can follow.

The ideal classroom is an interesting, lively and accepting place, where children are encouraged to ask their own questions and find out things for themselves, and where their efforts are valued by both the teacher and the other children. Here, mistakes are seen as steps towards independence, not as errors to be instantly corrected. Here, what children have learned at home exists comfortably alongside what they learn at school.

The Reading Environment

Much of what young children have learned at home is first-hand experience of the world, fashioned out of their own questions and interests. But most of them have also experienced the world through their imaginations. They have listened to stories, said poems, and shared books with others. Through seeing adults reading a variety of materials for particular purposes (timetables, recipes, advertisements, posters), children have begun to realise that reading can lead them not only into the world of imagination, but that it has a very practical function in everyday life. At school, an accepting teacher and an environment that is alive with print can stimulate these ideas.

A rich reading environment stimulates ideas about the functions of print.

54

Children have a natural desire to learn to read. A print-rich school and class environment is an ideal place in which all kinds of reading can flourish. Books, notices, posters, labels, children's own writings, pictures with captions, *Ready to Read* nursery rhyme charts, duty lists, messages, reminders, a list of TV programmes, words of songs, other children's names—on labels, drawings, and exercise books—are all around. Print leaps out at the children. It's there on the blackboard, on the walls, on the classroom door, on the nature table, on their lunch boxes, on the school-bus, in the car park, in the library, on the notice the children put in their school-bags to take home. To a large extent, this kind of environment determines the reading programme. A thoughtful teacher capitalises on opportunities to focus on such print and make children aware of its various functions in real contexts.

Reading flourishes where there is plenty to read.

The Way Environment Affects the Programme

For many teachers, the print-saturated environment may solve the problem of "what to do with the others" by providing the best reading activity of all—enjoyable, purposeful reading. For, given the choice of their own reading activity, children will make the most of their opportunities. Some will lie in the book corner and read a well-known book; some will join a friend to read a familiar nursery rhyme, pointing to the text as they do so. Others may prefer to read to each other, to write something in the writing corner, to sit in an old armchair and listen to a taped story, to try out a new book of jokes, or to join a group reading a familiar story from the OHP.

A rich reading environment solves the problem of "what to do with the others".

While these valuable experiences are taking place, the teacher moves around among the individuals and groups, reading along with some, sharing an exciting story, acknowledging some children's attempts at reading, asking questions of others to lead them closer to the meaning, or helping the diffident to find something of interest to read or a group to join. She works in a concentrated way with children grouped for guided reading, or takes a running record with an individual. This kind of environment gives her the chance to work with children as individuals. It gives the children the chance to learn to read the way adults read—for a real and satisfying purpose. As Margaret Meek says:

> Reading is whole-task learning, right from the start. From first to last, the child should be invited to behave like a reader, and those who want to help him should assume that he can learn and will learn, just as happened when he began to talk.*

*Margaret Meek in *Learning to Read*. The Bodley Head, 1982, p. 24.

The Idea of Balance

In children's first few years at school, teachers aim to develop the attitudes, understandings, and strategies outlined in chapters 2 and 3. No one way of teaching reading or single set of materials will be sufficient to achieve these purposes. This view is based on the belief that children benefit in different ways, and in different degrees, from a particular reading experience. Teachers need, therefore, to move away from a single approach which assumes that all children must move forward in a lockstep fashion. As they get to know their children and monitor their learning progress, teachers will be able to combine various approaches, described in this chapter, sometimes within a lesson, or within a day, as well as within the broader programme.

A reading-language programme should be balanced and varied.

Many junior class teachers in New Zealand have been given guidance on using various approaches to teaching reading through *ERIC* (the *Early Reading In-Service Course*). The following diagram, adapted from *ERIC*, shows how the approaches which comprise a balanced programme assist children in their growth towards independence in reading during the first three years at school.

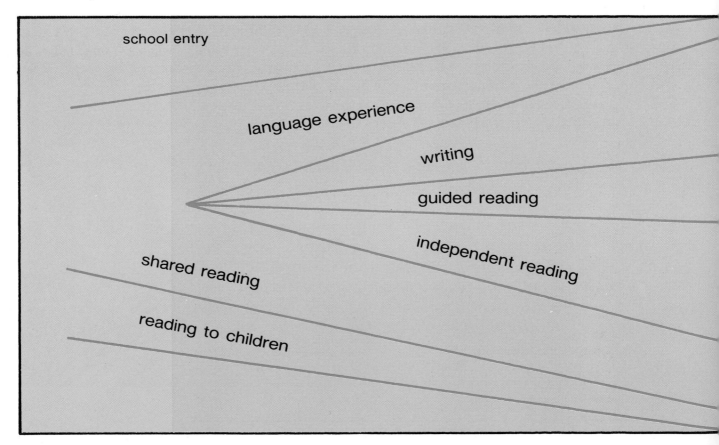

school entry

language experience

writing

guided reading

independent reading

shared reading

reading to children

The Major Approaches

1. *Reading to Children*

Reading from the best of the many children's books now available should be a daily part of any junior school reading programme. Taking time to be seen reading with enjoyment, or to read aloud to children, demonstrates, in the most direct way possible, a teacher's belief that reading is important, that books are a source of delight, and can, for example, help people come to grips with their emotions. Reading to children also familiarises them with book language and story structure, as well as introducing them to new words and ideas;* it builds a background of book experience which children can draw on as they learn to read independently. Hearing many stories read or told is a particularly valuable experience for children with little pre-school experience of books, and for those with English as a second language. From hearing good books read aloud, children can learn a great deal about the nature of reading while experiencing the rewards it can bring. Teachers should not feel that reading good books aloud to children is a waste of time.

> **Through hearing stories read, and seeing other people read with pleasure, children discover the delights of reading.**

> **Reading to children is not a waste of time.**

2. *Shared Reading*

In their pre-school years, most children have learnt that stories, songs, and poems are a source of delight. Through hearing stories read again and again, they have become familiar with the sound of the language used in books, sometimes memorising the repetitive parts of the text. They have learnt to listen attentively, to predict happenings in a story, and to enjoy a sense of satisfaction as the story unfolds.

Most new entrant children are familiar with some of the conventions of print through their pre-school experience. These learnings have been absorbed, not through systematic instruction, but in the course of sharing books with an adult in a warm and reassuring setting. Through such shared experiences, children enrich their understandings of the world and build up a reservoir of knowledge on which future understandings will be based.

Intuitively, many parents have stimulated a delight in reading by sharing this experience, helping the child to identify with the characters in stories and with their actions, talking about the pictures, and encouraging, predicting, joining in, singing along or chanting refrains. Children with such a background of rich book experience are well on the way

> **Shared reading builds on pre-school experience of books.**

> **Shared reading lays the foundations for reading for oneself.**

*This has been confirmed by Warwick Elley in a recent (1983) study in Christchurch schools. See "What Do Children Learn from Being Read To?" in *Set* number one, 1985, item 11. NZCER and ACER, 1985.

to becoming readers, and will approach school reading with an expectation that it will be absorbing and relevant. They will also have confidence in their ability to learn to read.

The benefits of bringing similar sharing procedures into the classroom were recognised by Don Holdaway in the 1960s. Working with a group of Auckland teachers, he explored the possibility of enriching existing programmes by incorporating repetitive stories, songs, and chants. The programmes, techniques, and styles of teaching came to be loosely bound together under the term "shared book experience". (This was often done using enlarged texts.) Many other terms have been used to refer to methods of supporting children by reading *with* them. These include, "read-along", "co-operative" reading, "assisted" reading, "unison", "choral", and "shared" reading.

Shared reading experience has various names.

The main idea behind all these approaches is that of support for children. This support will ensure that the children can enjoy material that they cannot as yet read for themselves, and appreciate the story as a whole, in much the same way as a completed picture in a jigsaw means more than any individual piece. Children can also be introduced to the riches of book language, and given shared opportunities to develop the strategies of sampling, predicting, confirming, and self-correcting for future independent use. Most important of all, children can enjoy the same sense of wonder, satisfaction, and comfort they felt when they were read stories at bedtime.

The main purpose of shared reading is support for the child.

These outcomes, however, exist only if the best books, which stand up to repeated readings, are chosen.

It is only the best books we want to read time and again.

58

Shared Reading of a New Story

The initial sharing of a new story is done as the teacher reads it *at one sitting* to the children. But, before reading begins, the teacher would probably "tune the children in" to the story, perhaps referring to the title, the characters, the illustrations, and the possible events but *without disclosing the story-line.* Looking at all the pictures, for instance, before the children read the story, may take away the point of reading it. For example, using the *Ready to Read* book, *Shopping with a Crocodile*, the teacher might say:

> Here's our old friend the crocodile.
>
> Where else have we met him?
>
> How can we be sure it's the same crocodile?
>
> What's he doing?
>
> Yes. It does look as though he's off to the shops.
>
> Is he pleased to be going or not?
>
> What do you think might happen to him at the shops?
>
> I'll read you the story and we'll see if we were right.

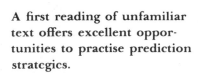

The teacher then reads through the story, shows and discusses the pictures, and asks the children to suggest outcomes and events. Throughout this first reading, the teacher is alert to possible misunderstandings and confusions, and untangles these as the sharing proceeds. This first sharing of unfamiliar text takes advantages of the chance to work on strategies and provides the best opportunity for children to use their knowledge of both language and the world around them to predict words and likely events. As their competence grows, children can also make use of their knowledge of letter-sound relationships to assist them in confirming or correcting their predictions. But the prime purpose of this first reading is to present the story as a story, to build up a lively interest in the reading, and to have fun.

Further Sharing of the Same or Other Stories

The subsequent rereading of the story, if both children and teacher are eager to return to it, may be done in a variety of ways. Enjoyment must always be paramount, but teachers may choose to focus on particular aspects, for example, in *Shopping with a Crocodile,* direct speech (*Who is speaking now?*), or unfamiliar vocabulary ("hesitate", "grumpily", "beckons"). These further explorations of a story* may be done in any of the following ways. Remember that selection is important. Teachers need to take care not to do a story to death.

***

*Examples are taken from the *Ready to Read* series.

Sharing a new story should be done at one sitting, and at a good pace.

Tuning in to a new story doesn't mean giving its point away.

A first reading of unfamiliar text offers excellent opportunities to practise prediction strategics.

Practising reading strategies should not interfere with the pace and fun of shared reading.

Teachers should return to books for further sharings only if children want to.

A story can be killed if it is used for excessive teaching.

- The children may listen to the teacher read the story and join in with familiar or repetitive sections, for example, ". . . and that was the end of that!" (*Greedy Cat*)

- The teacher may read the story with the children and invite them to chant a refrain, following on the enlarged sections she has previously prepared or written on the blackboard. For example, using *The Biggest Cake in the World* and picking up the refrain: "Mrs Delicious got a truck full of flour for the biggest cake in the world. Mrs Delicious got a tank full of milk for . . ."

- Teachers may use an enlarged text, either commercially produced or of their own making, and encourage the children to read it in unison. Although opportunities may be taken to attend to word and letter details, this should not distract from the enjoyment or understanding of the story as a whole. The use of an enlarged text is a step towards children returning to the "small" version of the story for independent reading.

- The teacher and children may read in unison from individual copies. If appropriate, the children's attention may be drawn to book or print conventions, or to word or letter details.

- Children may listen to the taped version of the story and "read along", endeavouring to match the words they see with the words they hear.
- Children may listen several times at intervals to the taped version of a story, and then attempt to read the story for themselves.

By sharing stories with children in many ways, teachers can tease out understandings and make the books so familiar that most of the children will be able to read them for themselves.

3. *Language Experience*

Language helps to make sense of experience, and children need conversations with an interested adult to stretch their minds and lift their language to a higher level of functioning. The language experience approach helps children to develop their language through diverse experiences in which speaking and listening are enriched through exploring, thinking, and feeling. These activities lead on naturally to writing and reading. With the teacher's help, children record experiences and ideas of their own, in their own words. These are then worked into text which they are able to read.

The language experience approach helps children record their own experiences in their own words.

Reading back their own words makes reading especially meaningful for children.

> Experience—spoken language—written language—reading—rereading.
> This is the pattern of language experience work.

What Experiences Can Be Used?

Talking, writing, and reading can be based on common school experiences—a field trip, a visitor to the classroom, a play, or an experiment—as well as on individual and personal experiences to do with people, friends, or family. Because the talking and writing are products of each child's thoughts about their own world, they have special meaning. Children can talk not only about what *has* happened to them, but what is going to happen, or what might happen, or what might have happened if things had turned out differently.

The kinds of experiences which can be used are personal and group.

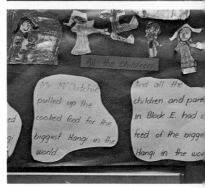

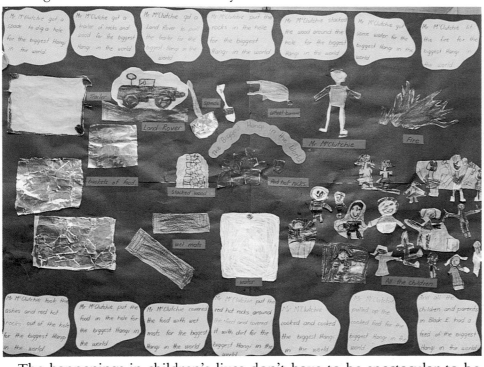

The happenings in children's lives don't have to be spectacular to be interesting. A child's widening world is full of new things to do and see. Pearl Arano describes a small Maori girl and her grandmother:

Nana was going to pick puha; the mokopuna decided to go, too.
"Are we going a long way, Nana?"
"Is Mummy bringing the lunch?"
"You know how to pick, Nana?"
"Help get things ready. What things, Nana?"

   Together Te Atawhai and Nana measured out a cup of flour and a quarter of a teaspoonful of salt into a plastic bag. They wrapped the sharp spatula-shaped knife in a clean sugar bag and placed all in a kete Maori.
"Tupu make this knife, eh Nana?"
"Oops, it's sharp!"
"What's matches for, eh? *You* don't smoke Nana, and why's the cardboard?"

62

"A surprise; *I likes surprise.*"

All was ready: off they went down through the house paddock, heading towards the creek. Te Atawhai saw some flowers; she picked some and brought them to Nana.

"See Nana, yellow flowers. What's theys called?"

"Dan-da-lines! Dan-da-lines! Dan-da-lines!"

"They's got a big sound likes me."

"They's not big likes me."*

Other people's words can also be an experience for us. Books and their language are part of language experience as well as the product of it. Children can innovate on book language, retelling a story in a new form by keeping to the original structures but inserting new vocabulary. This part modelling, part creating is a useful step in understanding how written language works and the many relationships between words and people.

Language experience includes making use of other people's language patterns.

The Teacher's Role in Language Experience

The teacher's main function in language experience is to extend a child's command of language. The quality of the child's talk is determined by the nature of the experience and the exchanges between teacher and child.

The teacher's main function in language experience is to extend the child's command of language.

Teachers need to be sensitive to children's efforts to express themselves. Sometimes the teacher could encourage children to reflect on their own comments, inviting them to offer more. She or he may rephrase the children's responses in such a way that it draws out further

The ways of drawing out responses and responding vary according to situation and culture.

---

*From an unpublished manuscript, "Playing, Learning, and Growing with Natural Materials", by Pearl Arano, 1984.

thought and communication: "Yes, that certainly does seem a dangerous place for a cat to be!" Sometimes the teacher is a sounding board, and a nod of agreement is a more appropriate response, giving children more time to find the confidence to speak, to consider what they are saying. This allows them to elaborate without prompting. Teachers should also be aware of cultural differences. In some cultures, silence represents agreement, in others disagreement.*

It is essential that the teacher's invitations to respond don't restrict the children to producing predetermined answers, but draw out as much as possible from the experience involved. Comments such as, "Tell me about . . .", "What would happen if . . .?", "How did you . . . ?", or "Do you think . . . ?" are likely to help children to think and respond in their own ways. If the teacher continues to talk with the child in ways that do not seem to demand "correct" answers, the child's confidence in responding will grow.

Marie Clay comments:

When we try to provide experiences that will compensate for poor language backgrounds, we must go beyond the usual bounds of spontaneous learning in a free play situation or group learning from one teacher. The child's spontaneous wish to communicate about something which interests him at one particular moment should have priority and he must have adults who will talk with him, in simple, varied and grammatical language. We should arrange for language-producing activities where adult and child must communicate to co-operate.**

Self-Worth and Non-Standard English
By not immediately correcting to standard forms what children offer, the teacher demonstrates an acceptance of the children themselves. Implying that a child's language is inferior implies that the child is inferior, too. But what does a teacher do when a child wants to write, "I didn't have no lunch money."? If the teacher's purpose is primarily to show children the one-to-one matching of the spoken word with its written symbol, she will record the child's words exactly, or she will assist the child to write down these words just as they were spoken. If children already have this important understanding about reading, she can tactfully extend their grasp of the varieties of English by helping them rephrase their words in standard English. Marie Clay says:

Adults need to talk with children in ways that help them respond in their own words and, at the same time, help children elaborate their ideas.

What children can say, they can write; what they can write, they can read.

---

*See pages 20–22 in *Talking Past Each Other* by Joan Metge and Patricia Kinloch. Victoria University Press, 1978.
**Marie Clay in *Reading: The Patterning of Complex Behaviour*. Heinemann Educational Books, 2nd ed., 1979, pp. 53–4.

For the non reader, his own language patterns should be a guide to the type of text he should try to read until the reading process is well-established. Meantime, his oral control over language can receive attention so that it develops not from his reading but in parallel with it.*

Children's Own Text and Early Reading

Text which children have produced out of their own experience in familiar language patterns makes good emergent and early reading material. "What the child can produce, he can also anticipate. This . . . gives him time to attend to cues, and to relate several cues to one another."**

Children's own text, based on their own language, feelings and thoughts is not necessarily bland or colourless—the language structures and vocabulary used may be more lively than that found in many supplementary readers. For example, from a five-year-old: "I spent my lunch money on Space Invaders, and Jimmy gave me a sandwich, but I was ravenous when I got home."

Children's own language is usually concrete and vivid.

Language Experience and Variety of Text

As language experience text is closely related to the child's world outside as well as inside school, the resulting stories take many forms—charts, labels, speech "balloons", wall stories, captions for photographs, diaries, audio tapes with accompanying booklets, interest dictionaries, shopping lists, dialogue, prose, and even poetry. Children become familiar in this way with the many varieties of language form and use. This is of special value to children who are learning English as a second language.

---

*Marie Clay in *Reading: The Patterning of Complex Behaviour.* Heinemann Educational Books, 2nd ed., 1979, p. 70.
**Marie Clay, (as above) 1972 ed., p. 33.

The following running record shows a child drawing on an experience outside school to solve a problem.

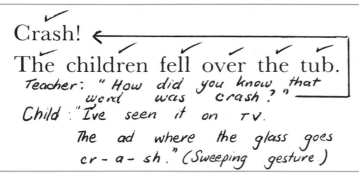

Crash!
The children fell over the tub.

Teacher: "How did you know that word was crash?"
Child: "I've seen it on TV. The ad where the glass goes cr-a-sh." (Sweeping gesture)

Language experience also makes children familiar with many of the conventions of print in contexts which are directly relevant to the children's interests. Through this approach, children come to a realisation of their role as both the producers and interpreters of the written word and of the inter-relationships between listening, talking, writing, and reading.

Many varieties of language and many print conventions are learned through language experience.

Language Experience and ESL Children
Depending on the stage the children have reached, the teacher will either write down what is offered, or encourage the children to do this for themselves. This demonstrates acceptance of the children, which is especially important for those who are learning English as a second language. But these children obviously need help to produce grammatically accurate structures. The sensitive teacher will know whether non-standard forms reflect varieties of English, or result from limited knowledge of language structures and vocabulary. Here, putting words into chil-

The teacher writes down what is offered or encourages children to do this for themselves.

On Monday, I Watch goody goody yum yum. When is finish. And I go to Sleep With my Mother my Father. When is morning I go to School. With myself.

dren's mouths takes on a different aspect. Many of the benefits of language experience remain the same for all children, but in particular second language learners improve because:

- Talking over what happens during and following an experience increases the children's understanding of it and its associated language.
- Drawing on experiences of particular cultural significance means the teacher can provide material that is appropriate and meaningful for the children to read.
- Talking over what is to be written and observing the children's attempts to master the reading and writing task gives the teacher valuable insights not only into children's learning but also into the children themselves.
- Reading material which they have produced in collaboration with the teacher helps children and teacher share a common background for understanding. Here the teacher can show her respect for other views of the world.

Sylvia Ashton-Warner writes of her own language experience teaching:

> Back to these first words. To these first books. They must be made out of the stuff of the child itself. I reach a hand into the mind of the child, bring out a handful of the stuff I find there, and use it as our first working material. Whether it is good or bad stuff, violent or placid stuff, coloured or dun. To effect an unbroken beginning. And in this dynamic material, within the familiarity and security of it, the Maori finds that words have intense meaning to him, from which cannot help but arise a love of reading. For it's here, right in this first word, that the love of reading is

Language experience is especially beneficial for children learning English as a second language.

67

born, and the longer his reading is organic the stronger it becomes, until by the time he arrives at the books of the new culture, he receives them as another joy rather than as a labour. I know all this because I've done it.*

A Language Experience Session

One teacher's language experience session followed this pattern. It is one of many possible variants.

- The teacher capitalises on a child's interests and experiences, encourages the child to talk about them, and enhances understanding through the use of questions which sharpen thought or language.

The child's interests and experiences are used.

- Much of this talk may arise from something the child has done, drawn, made, or painted, and the child may be eager for the teacher to help record an experience in writing. The teacher can ask the child, "What do you want to say about it? What will you write? Do you need any help?"

- The teacher may sometimes write the child's words under the child's picture, or label a model. By doing this, the teacher helps the child discover that it is possible to communicate through marks on paper. The concept that thoughts and speech can be represented by writing, is one which the child may not have grasped, just as children often do not realise what adults are actually doing when they say they are reading. For many a child, the adult is just staring at a newspaper instead of paying attention to the real world!

The child is helped to discover that marks on paper communicate ideas.

*Sylvia Ashton Warner in *Teacher*. Secker and Warburg, 1963, p.34.

- Many children from the start want to write something for themselves. Some might attempt their own names, while others might pick out a few familiar letters and write these several times—gradually building up confidence in using a pencil. Children should be encouraged to write some or most of their story for themselves.

- All these stories are relevant to the children concerned, and they will enjoy having the stories read to them, reading them with someone, taking them home to read, and rereading them themselves at a later date.

4. *Guided Reading*

Guided reading is an approach which enables a teacher and a group of children to talk, read, and think their way purposefully through a text, making possible an early introduction to reading silently. Most of our lives, we read silently, and for a reason.

Stimulating children's interest comes first, and the techniques of guided reading enable the teacher, from the beginning, to involve children in wondering what will happen next, to respond to ideas, and to identify with situations and characters in books. In this way, children come to know reading as a process of actively reconstructing meaning, and not as a recitation of words. It is a process of predicting one's way through print.

In the course of guided reading lessons, when a stumbling block to comprehension occurs, the teacher is often able to identify children's needs and to provide appropriate teaching, either there and then, or in subsequent lessons. In essence, a teacher using the approach well, is developing the attitudes, understandings, and strategies that will make children well motivated and independent readers.

> [Guided] silent reading enables the reader to apply the skills he is learning, and the teacher to find out how effectively these are being used, and what further teaching and practice are needed. This is part of the plan to convince him he *can* cope with difficulties.*

Before the Reading — Choosing a Text

Having decided on the purpose(s) for reading, the teacher selects a text which is interesting, manageable in length, and at an appropriate level of challenge for the group. The challenge may lie less in the text than in the ideas presented. Children "must expect both to meet difficulties and to be able to overcome them",** but if there are too many, comprehension becomes difficult and interest is lost. Reading should never become a struggle. Teachers should err on the side of selecting books that are too easy rather than too difficult, especially when the ideas they convey are hard to grasp.

A guided reading text should not present too many and too varied difficulties.

*Reading Suggestions for Teaching Children with Reading Difficulties in Primary and Secondary Schools. Department of Education, 1978, p. 44.
**Reading: Suggestions for Teaching Reading in Primary and Secondary Schools. Department of Education, 1972, p. 116.

Before the Reading—Selecting a Purpose

The teacher needs to be clear about the purpose for reading. Often the purpose will be simply to ensure that the children enjoy a story, teasing out the text to enhance appreciation of plot and characters. Sometimes it will be to teach or reteach strategies, so that children can overcome difficulties in working towards meaning. On other occasions, a simple study skill, such as using a table of contents (as in any of the *Ready to Read* miscellanies) or using pictures to gather information may be taught. (An example from the *Ready to Read* series is "Crossing Water" in *Horrakapotchkin!*) But such teaching should be a means only to children's enjoyment and understanding, and relate only to what they need to know to make sense of what they are reading.

Introducing the Reading

Once the purpose for reading has been decided, the teacher prepares the children for what is to come.

The opening discussion usually stems from a recent experience or topic of interest, from the title of a story, the illustrations, author, chief characters, place names, or from reading the opening lines of the text.

By the time they begin to read any particular part of the full text independently, the children should:

- Know that the reading will inform or entertain them.
- Have certain questions in mind which they expect the text to answer.
- Have some knowledge of how to cope with the difficulties they will encounter.
- Feel eager to get under way.

What is to be done about new words? This depends on the language and background experience children bring to the text. It also depends on whether the words in question are related to new ideas which the text itself will make clear as the story unfolds. Teaching new words ahead of time robs children of the chance to meet and overcome difficulties for themselves, but potentially difficult concepts which must be understood before the reading can make sense should be talked over first. Myrtle Simpson points out:

> Even teachers who have niggling doubts about the wisdom of teaching words ahead continue to follow this practice because it appears to produce results quickly. Some feel that it gives them, as well as the children, a sense of security. They forget that it also makes children unwilling to face the hazard of a new book: in short, teaching words ahead produces dependent rather than independent readers.*

---

*Myrtle Simpson in *Suggestions for Teaching Reading in Infant Classes*. Department of Education, 1962, p.42.

The purpose for reading determines the way children are helped to understand and enjoy the text.

An introduction should engage the children's interest and make the purposes for reading clear.

Introducing any new words or concepts is done only as much as is necessary to establish meaning.

71

During the Reading

Initially, with very young children, the reading will be of small sections of the text, possibly with the teacher reading a sentence or two, discussing this, encouraging predictions, then asking the children "to read with their eyes" to confirm their suggestions. The children may be asked to retell a part in their own words, to share some parts aloud in unison, or to read a section aloud to prove a point raised in discussion. As time passes, children are able to read increasingly longer sections silently until, for example, whole *Ready to Read* stories become manageable as guided reading. The discussion which the teacher initiates during reading should never interfere with understanding and enjoyment. Properly done, it brings children to the stage where they enter into the kind of dialogue with the author independently, reading like mature readers for understanding and personal satisfaction.

Guided reading enables children to practise strategies with the teacher's support, and leads to independent silent reading.

After the Reading

What happens after reading will be determined by the nature of the text, the children's responses to it, and the purpose the teacher had in mind. Often the reading is sufficient in itself, particularly if the children have been talking about characters, ideas, or events, and predicting and confirming their understandings of the text. Comprehension, for them, should be something that happens *as* they read and not as something that comes as a result of writing answers to written questions later on.

Children should never come to think of reading as the time when they do "busy-work" exercises. Some related activities may offer useful practice of skills taught during or immediately after reading, but primarily the best activity for children becoming good at reading is to do a great deal of it. Most of all, children need many suitable books and the time to read them in.

"Busy work" is often pointless.

Maui and his brothers are catching the sun.

Asking Questions

As well as being good observers and good listeners, teachers need to be good questioners.*

Sometimes there is a place for not asking a question at all, but for starting the talking by stating a point of view, suggesting a hypothesis, or simply nodding in encouragement. But as questioning remains the prevailing way of getting a discussion going, teachers should be clear about their purpose for asking questions before they pose them.

Teachers need to be clear about the point of the questions they ask.

A major difference in questions is between closed and open-ended questions. Closed questions have a particular answer. Open-ended questions have many possible answers. Closed questions ask children to search

Closed and open-ended questions demand different kinds of answers.

*Refer to the extended discussion on teachers' questioning techniques in *Young Children Learning: Talking and Thinking at Home and at School* by Barbara Tizard and Martin Hughes. Fontana Paperbacks, 1984, pp. 188–213.

73

for facts, often stated in the text. Open-ended questions ask for inferences or hypotheses. The distinction between questions whose answers are to be found in, or inferred from, the text should be made clear to the child. Teachers should direct the child, where appropriate, to "look at the text and tell me . . ."

Tell children if closed or open-ended questions relate to the text.

Introducing a Story by Questions

When a story is being introduced, discussion is often initiated to build up background experience. Here, a teacher might first ask closed questions, relating to prior knowledge,* such as:

> Do you know how beekeepers catch bees? *(Nana's in the Plum Tree)*
> What is a tuatara? *(Old Tuatara)*
> Where have we met this crocodile before? (The *Crocodile* Series)
> Can you ride a bike? *(My Bike)*
> Have you ever seen a bird's nest in a tree? *(Blackbird's Nest)*
> Have you ever seen a bird building its nest? *(Blackbird's Nest)*

But the teacher might have a different purpose—to make the children want to read the story, to tune them in to its mood and content, and to stir imagination. Here, open-ended questions might be used. For example:

> Where do you think the taniwha might be? *(Where's the Taniwha?)*
> What sort of boots do you think Toots would like? *(Boots for Toots)*
> Who do you think will need to be rescued? *(The Rescue)*
> Why do you think he's called a "greedy cat"? *(Greedy Cat)*
> What do you think he has got to grumble about? *(The Great Grumbler)*

Note that the children are being asked all the time to speculate, to think, and to imagine. This is of particular use in prediction, where background experience is used to make enlightened guesses about the unknown.

Questions During the Reading

During the reading session, questions asked will be designed to guide the children through the text, to set a purpose for reading further, to focus children's attention on meaning, to draw attention to details in illustrations and text, and to help children overcome difficulties. These will usually be closed questions, for example:

> Look at the text on those two pages again. What things has Matthew already read? *(Matthew Likes to Read)*
> Look at page seventeen. Why did Mum think Uncle Joe got fat? *(Uncle Joe)*
> How many eggs does the text tell us are there? *(Blackbird's Nest)*

---

*Examples are taken from the *Ready to Read* series.

Can you find the word that tells you what the eggs looked like? (Blackbird's Nest)

Look at the text on the next page. What does it say about how Nana got the bees into the box? (Nana's in the Plum Tree)

Read that page to yourself. Who else came into the big bed? (The Big Bed)

The answers to some inferential questions are also related to specific points of the text. Children whose inferences are off the track should be redirected to the words. Examples are:

Did the milkman drop any bottles? Yes, he stopped "with a crash and a splash". (Number One)

Is Hine still frightened of the bees? Yes, because she "watched from a long way off". (Nana's in the Plum Tree)

Closed questions can relate to particular features of print, for example:

What made you go back and change your mind about that word?

How can you be sure that that word is "dinner"?

But to encourage children to think "beyond" the text, the teacher will need to ask open-ended questions that often have more than one answer. Such questions help children to identify with the events and characters in the story, and help them to think about the deeper layers of meaning in the story, for example:

Why do you think she felt shy with him? (Paul)

What would it be like to be physically handicapped? (Paul)

What other stories do you know where people help each other like this? (Paul)

Each child in the group needs an opportunity to answer questions. If the same few vocal and confident children answer all questions, the rest will come to rely on these few, and fail to take a full part in the lesson.

Teachers need to ensure that they do not dismiss children's answers merely because they do not exactly correspond with their own pre-conceived "correct" answer. The children's answers may be "right" in their own terms, and such answers may give the teacher insights into the child's own understandings, background experience, and method of processing print.

Unanticipated answers are not necessarily wrong.

5. *Independent Reading*

Young children need support and encouragement in their early efforts to read. They should, however, be able to gain some measure of independence at all levels. The independent reading of books, labels, letters, print of all sorts, is an integral part of a reading programme and should not be seen as separate from it. Every child should have time to read suitable materials independently every day.

Children should be able to gain a measure of independence at all levels.

75

Sometimes the teacher will select the material for the children to read independently, and sometimes the independent reading of books will spontaneously follow a shared or guided reading lesson. On most occasions, the children will choose their own books for independent reading from the range of appropriate materials in the book corner, in book boxes or hampers, or from the school library. Most children will select so-called "easy" reading to confirm their success as readers, but others may need help to choose appropriate books. Some children don't persevere with books they have chosen themselves. They may have been attracted by a bright cover or illustrations, only to discover later that the text is too difficult to read.

After children have read a story independently, the teacher could discuss the favourite or "puzzling" parts with them. She or he might ask them if they have enjoyed the book and would like to reread it sometime, whether they have read other books by the same author, how these books compare with the one they've read, or how any film or TV version compares, or what they have understood about the story.

Wide easy reading gives the children the chance to practise their reading strategies on familiar and, occasionally, on unfamiliar materials. "Clocking up reading mileage" makes skilled, independent readers. Quiet time, during which all children read silently, may be the only opportunity for uninterrupted reading in a busy and noisy day.

There should be time each day for independent reading.

Clocking up reading mileage on easy material is one of the most important aspects of independent reading.

The Teacher's Role in Independent Reading

Teachers can learn a great deal about children's reading progress by observing their independent reading behaviour. They might ask themselves these questions. Does the child:

- Consistently choose books that present too many difficulties, or restrict his or her choice to books that present few challenges?
- Enjoy returning again and again to familiar and well-loved stories?
- Become absorbed in stories or just flip pages aimlessly?
- Make use of the illustrations or just give them a cursory glance?
- Seek help immediately when meeting a difficulty or try to overcome it without help?

The insights gained through such observations can be used in planning a balanced reading programme.

The insights gained through a teacher's monitoring of children's independent reading can be used in planning a balanced programme.

Using the School Library

Many children have been used to visiting a public library before they start school. All children should be introduced to the school library as soon as possible.

The library should be a friendly, exciting, and comfortable place. Teachers should help children to feel at home there and show them how to make the best use of its books and other resources.

Children should feel at home in the school library.

The school library is a place for sharing. Children can make a contribution by having their drawings or the items they have collected displayed. They can take part in talking about stories or in telling stories to others. They can help to set out or tidy library materials.

The library contributes by:

- Having good picture books for sharing in the library or for borrowing.
- Holding story-telling sessions by teachers, authors, or older children.
- Having well-illustrated books on such topics of interest to young readers as other countries, animals, and sports.
- Having a listening post, picture collection, and other material to support reading.
- Making a quiet place available for "a good read".

Children will need regular, consistent help in how to make the best use of library resources, especially in how to:

Children need regular and consistent help to make the best use of the school library.

- Browse through shelves and displays.
- Choose appropriate books for recreation or information.
- Understand how the materials are arranged on the shelves.
- Find books by authors, titles, or subjects.
- Use the listening post or pictures to enrich their enjoyment.

School policy should give teachers the opportunity to open up the library to all children from new entrants upwards. The School Library Service *Manual for School Libraries, 1984* sets out objectives for the library. School Library Service advisers can assist schools with particular policy development.

6. *Writing**

Writing and reading are associated processes.

Writing should be part of a balanced reading and language programme. Regular opportunities should be provided for children to produce their own written material which can then be read to others or by them. In the course of writing many drafts, children learn much about reading and writing. Teachers should encourage these approximations and not expect perfection at a first attempt.

There is a reciprocal relationship between reading and writing: both are concerned with meaning and each one has its own special characteristics. The *reader* reconstructs meaning from the symbols on the page, attending only to enough of the details of print to ensure understanding. The *writer*, on the other hand, starts with ideas and has to represent

---

*This section is not intended to be comprehensive, as much attention is currently being given to the place of writing in a reading-language programme in New Zealand schools.

these with symbols, using appropriate literary style to suit the intended audience. A child who has worked hard to establish meaning in a personal piece of writing is well equipped to search for meaning in the writings of others. A method employed by Margaret Meek is to persuade the child to tell a story, the gist of which is written down by the teacher. The teacher and child then work together to polish drafts of the story, which is eventually read out loud.

While children write, they are also practising many of the skills of reading.

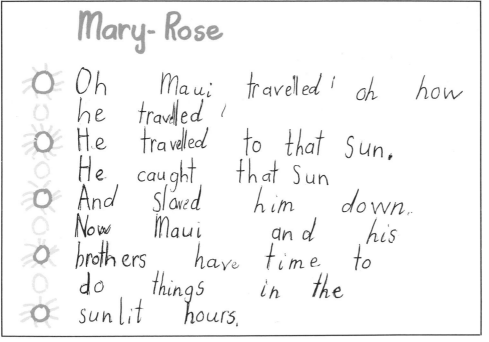

Mary-Rose

Oh Maui travelled! oh how he travelled!
He travelled to that sun.
He caught that sun
And slowed him down.
Now Maui and his brothers have time to do things in the sunlit hours.

On the stones
There he lives
Beside the stream
There he lives
Near the bush
There he lives

Beneath the sun
There he lies
Watching the gulls
There he lies
Near the sea and the gentle w
He listens and watches and catches flies

Many complementary skills and understandings are gained through reading and writing. Children confirm that written text makes sense because, in producing their own writing, they have had to make their ideas into sense for others. Writing also crystallises for many children their concepts of a word, a sentence, and a letter. It reinforces their understanding of the one-to-one relationship between spoken and written words, but also makes them more aware of the different styles of speech and writing. Other complementary understandings are:

• Sounds can be associated with the symbols that represent them.
• The sequences of the sounds of spoken words relate to the left to right sequences in written words.
• The directional rules and conventions of written English are consistent.
• There are consistencies in spelling.
• Relationships of form and meaning exist between new words and words already known.
• Paying attention to how to write a word helps in recognising it later.

Evaluation

A well-balanced reading and language programme is flexible enough to cater for children of all ages and cultural backgrounds, for children of varying maturity, language development, interest, adjustment to school, and social and physical development.

We might ask these questions of any programme:

A well-balanced programme should provide for the diversity of the children it serves.

Attitudes and Opportunities

- Do the children have a growing interest in books and in writing?
- Does the programme allow for children to progress at different rates?
- Are there opportunities for children to speak, listen, read, write, interact, and so build up self-esteem through success?
- Are children encouraged to ask questions?

Resources

- Is there a good supply of easy reading material for children to choose from for independent reading?

Monitoring

- Is the teacher observing the progress children are making in situations other than during direct instruction?

Strategies

- Do the children constantly seek meaning from print, integrating their knowledge of the world, of the structure of language, and of the details of print?
- Do children demonstrate self-correcting behaviour regularly?

Parents

- Is there good liaison between home and school, so that parents are aware of the way reading is being taught in the school?

Cultural Diversity

- Are children's different social and cultural backgrounds being taken into account?

Teaching Approaches in a Balanced Reading Programme

Approach	Advantages	Limitations
Reading to Children	Familiarises children with the language and conventions of books. Helps children discover that books are worthwhile.	May reflect the teacher's interests rather than children's preferences. Does not allow for children to process print independently.
Language Experience	Child centred. Makes the connection between spoken and written forms of language. Offers familiar language. Provides meaningful text. Encourages memory for text.	Restricted to the child's spoken language. Does not give experience with book language.
Shared Reading	Offers rich book language, new vocabulary, and growing familiarity with conventions of written language. As with reading to children, gives access to interesting, lively literature that may be beyond children's present reading capabilities.	Some children may develop a memory for text, with little other basis for self-correction strategies.
Guided Reading	Deepens understandings of the text. Presents many opportunities for specific teaching as difficulties arise. Encourages silent reading.	Choice of text depends on the teacher's assessment of group capabilities and interests.
Independent Reading	Caters for individual abilities, interests. Opportunities to practise self-monitoring on real reading.	Children may choose books that are too difficult. Children may limit their choice to the same type of material.
Writing	Writing involves continuous reading. It develops understandings about visual cueing systems, e.g., grapho-phonic relationships, punctuation and other conventions. Semantic and syntactic prediction is high, increasing attention to checking and confirming. The child uses background knowledge and experience to compose meaningful text. See also Language Experience.	The child's imagination and knowledge are not enriched by the contents of good books, and by the range of forms and styles of book language. See also Language Experience.

5

The *Ready to Read* Series

The Original Series

The original *Ready to Read* Series was written to offer material which would provide a steady progression of difficulty for the teaching of reading to young children. The books were designed to enable beginning readers to make use of context through reading stories which were close to the experiences of New Zealand children, and which included language that they would use in conversation and hear in the stories read to them. The material was distributed free to all schools, thus catering for the mobility of teachers and children. It also provided a model for commercial publishers.

The handbook accompanying the original *Ready to Read* series, *Suggestions for Teaching Reading in Infant Classes* by Myrtle Simpson, emphasised that teaching should not precede the reading and that "reading must be easy enough for children to be able to discover unfamiliar words for themselves".* Teachers were encouraged to use a wide variety of books at each level to increase the children's confidence and independence, and to cater for varying rates of progress. The project also stressed the importance of relationships between teachers and children, and teachers and parents.

These principles have influenced the design of the revised series in intention, content, and format.

Major emphases in the original **Ready to Read** *series were grading, natural language, and relevant content.*

A variety of books and teaching methods was recommended. These led to independent reading.

The Revised Series

The series has been developed in response to two major impulses. Both of these derive from the experience teachers have had with the earlier version of the series, and from the evolving style of teaching reading in New Zealand. One is to foster an approach to teaching reading that builds on the children's spoken language, and on the experience of the world and books that they bring to school. The other is to publish books that can take their place alongside the best of children's picture books, and yet be part of a graded reading series.

New Zealand children in the past learned to read at school on books which often described the people and experiences of other countries. The original *Ready to Read* series attempted to redress this by reflecting the New Zealand scene. The revised series has portrayed New Zealand people and situations with greater realism, reflecting a diverse society.

There were two major impulses in the revised **Ready to Read** *series.*

---

*Myrtle Simpson in *Suggestions for Teaching Reading in Infant Classes*. Department of Education, 1962, p. 39.

83

It has also taken into account the interplay of fantasy and reality with which children experience the world.

The original *Ready to Read* series did not include material for the emergent reading stage. The revised series has filled this need by producing books which help children establish or confirm sound basic attitudes and understandings about reading.

Children have expectations of books based on their pre-school experiences.

Most children start school with certain expectations about books which relate to their pre-school experience of them. During this time, children have mostly been read to by competent readers—parents, older siblings, relations, friends, and other caring adults. They have come to associate books with times of being with another person during lulls in busy play, with widening horizons, and with the feelings of relaxation and security, say, at bedtime. Books themselves have come to be sources of stories, told in rhythms, colours, and forms that arouse curiosity, and excite, amuse, and delight. They are part of the serious business of play and the natural acquisition of language.

Reading at school should be entirely compatible with that kind of experience, and the books used for the teaching of reading should fulfil the children's expectations. The teacher should select books that match in quality the kind of books most children have come to love in their

Books at school should measure up to books read out of school.

pre-school years. As Margaret Meek says:

> If you want to make a reader, you have to find a book he can enjoy, one that makes him believe you think he can be a reader, and then you must help him to find his way through it.*

Principles Guiding the Development of the Revised Series

To achieve the intentions outlined above, the following principles have guided the development of the series.

Each text should have a strong story-line or plot. The chances for a child's successful progress through a structured series are greatly enhanced when the material is intrinsically interesting. In any story, the narrative itself should have sufficient impetus to take the reader to the end. Capturing the child's imagination provides the most effective motivation for reading.

Stories need a strong plot.

The text should present material close to the interests and experience of young children from a variety of cultural backgrounds, home circumstances, and locations.

The text should be able to take its place in a structured series. The nature and number of concepts and challenges in a story must match the child's developmental stage. The shape and style of the story must be appropriate for the content and concepts. The language should reflect the mood, plot, and content with simplicity and clarity.

Story content must be interesting, relevant, well shaped and expressed, and suited to children's development.

The books should look like books. They should follow book design, with a cover and a separate title page. They should be presented in a variety of formats, with a variety of type-faces and illustrative styles.

Books should look like books.

The illustrations should support and complement the text, and draw the child back into the story as well as extend imagination and understanding. The amount of text and illustration on any one opening, their placement in relationship to each other, the use of line breaks and space between lines, the weight of the type-face balanced against the size and style of the illustration, the space between words—these are all variables in presenting the author's message in the format most suitable for the reader.

Illustrations and typography should support and enhance the text.

Any series developed for a national education system should have an overall balance that reflects the diversity of make-up and experience to be found in the society the system serves. Cultural and social settings, locations, equal treatment of the sexes, a range of circumstances and

A national reading series should reflect the society in which it will be used.

---

*Margaret Meek in *Learning to Read*. The Bodley Head, 1982, p. 169.

roles at home and in the community, a range of emotional and social experience through fact and fiction—these are some of the components of that balance.

The material should be a flexible resource from which teachers can select and present books according to the interests, needs, and abilities of the children. Sometimes the teacher will present the text to the children, sharing it with them. At other times, the children will be encouraged to take more responsibility for getting the author's message either through guided or independent reading.

The Stages of Children's Reading Development

There are three broad stages of reading development: emergent, early, and fluency.

Emergent—Making a Start

The emergent reader has to learn "that a book is a special way of telling a story that lets the reader go back to it as often as he likes, that the words stay the same, that the pictures help the reader to understand the story, that the story has a shape and the author a voice."*

In addition to this, by the end of this stage, the reader should:
- Show interest in attempting to read the text unaided.
- Be able to consider what is read together with what is already known.
- Be able to discuss what is happening and what is likely to happen.
- Recognise a number of words in various contexts.

Pre-school experiences of books and print are extended at school as favourite books are revised and new ones introduced and shared.

Early—Becoming a Reader

This stage is critical in making sure that the habit of reading for meaning has been established. Children are encouraged to draw out meaning from text by becoming confident in:
- Using their background experience.
- Taking risks and making approximations.
- Using the text and illustrations to sample, predict, and confirm.
- Using letter-sound associations to confirm predictions.
- Using their knowledge of print conventions.
- Rerunning and reading on when they have lost the meaning.
- Self-correcting.
- Integrating strategies in a self-improving system.

---

*Margaret Meek in *Learning to Read.* The Bodley Head, 1982, p.66.

A reading series should be flexible enough to suit the diverse nature of children.

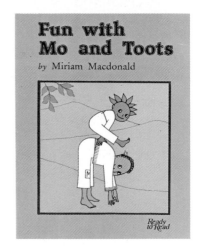

Emergent readers learn that books are a special and unchanging way of telling a story.

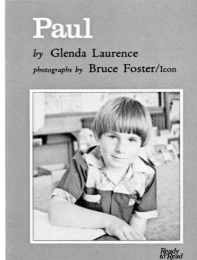

Establishing the habit of reading for meaning is essential in early reading.

As readers become fluent, attention to print details diminishes, and reading for a purpose determines the style and pace of reading.

Fluency—Going it Alone

What has been developed in the emergent and early stages is built on as the children increase in confidence and competence. The emphasis at this stage is on:

- Integrating cues.
- Reducing to a minimum attention to print detail.
- Maintaining meaning through longer and more complex sentence structures, various kinds of prose, and poetry.
- Adjusting the rate of reading to the purpose.

The Content of the Revised Series*

The revised *Ready to Read* series comprises:

- Some 40 single titles, including enlarged books, catering for the three broad stages of reading development, and graded into difficulty level within each stage.
- 7 miscellanies—collections of material of different kinds—graded as above.
- Enlarged poem cards, for use at all levels.
- 8 single titles, including one enlarged book, for sharing at all levels.
- 2 bilingual texts.
- A number of readalong cassettes.
- 1 pamphlet for parents.
- 1 take-home book for children starting school.
- 1 wall chart for teachers.
- 1 classified guide of complementary reading material.
- 1 handbook and related material for teachers.

The single titles and miscellanies are shown on pages 98–99. *They are listed in order of their increasing difficulty both within and between the levels, except for the first six titles in the emergent stage. These are designed for shared reading and may be taken in any order before the children are introduced to guided reading.* The titles of the other publications are also shown on pages 98–99.

*At the time of printing.

87

The Structure of the Revised Series in Relation to Grading

Children's growing competence in reading is catered for in books of increasing complexity and difficulty level. The material, therefore, is a graded series. At all times, however, the story has assumed the greatest importance. If a story is to merit the reader's time and attention, it must provide interest and excitement, and extend the imagination, as well as encourage further reading. The grading within the series has always been tempered by the needs of the story. Factors contributing to the grading included:

- Content.
- The children's assumed background experience.
- Story structure and style.
- Language structure.
- Vocabulary.
- Illustrations.
- Size and type of print.
- Amount, placement, and balance of illustrations and text.

Each item in the series was considered in relation to these factors individually and collectively, and as a single entity, as well as part of a series balanced in type, content, and format.

The Structure of the Series in Relation to Teaching Approach

Individual children approach books in different ways at different times. There are occasions when the child wants to read a book independently, while at other times the child needs help before a book can be enjoyed. *The books, therefore, are not designed to be used in only one way.* A particular book may be used for shared reading at one level of difficulty with one group of children, and for guided or independent reading at other levels. Whatever approach is used, the child should have continued access to the book and the amount of support required to enjoy the author's message. The emphasis should be on confirming and extending the child's experience and success with books and text, and on supporting the child towards independence.

Teachers, therefore, select a book bearing in mind these three main variables:

- The child's stage of reading development.
- The difficulty level of the book.
- The approach (shared, guided, or independent reading).

Each child's needs, experience, and interests vary; and, although books within each level of the *Ready to Read* series are graded in increasing difficulty, they *should not be used in an inflexible sequence.* What may be easy for one child may be difficult for another. Within each level, a change of approach will often affect the order in which books are used. A child at the fluency stage may even choose to return to emergent stage books for easy reading.

Most children will progress fairly evenly through the stages of reading development. This does not mean, however, that each child will systematically read every book in the *Ready to Read* series in a fixed order as shared, then guided and, finally, independent reading. It must be emphasised that:

- It is not absolutely necessary for every child to read every book in the series.
- Not every book will be used in all the ways suggested on the "colour wheel" (see below) in any one junior class or department.
- The books are not intended to be used in any *one* order.
- Teachers must not assume that each child should read a given book in the three different ways (as shared, guided, and independent reading).

Teachers will need to become familiar with the structure and content of the series in order to match the stage, level, and approach with books which suit each child's experience, abilities, interests, and needs.

The Colour Wheel

The flexible use of the *Ready to Read* books, and a guide to the stages, levels, and approaches which each one might be used for are indicated by a "colour wheel". This is printed on the back cover of each book. It offers guidance by matching the suggested approach with the appropriate stage and difficulty level. The suggested approaches for each book in the series are indicated in the outer ring of the colour wheel by the letter S (shared), G (guided), or I (independent), or, in the case of books for sharing at all levels, by an S in the centre of the wheel.

The sequence of colours on the wheel indicates the stages and difficulty levels, and remains constant throughout the series. (This sequence should be taken into account where printing procedures do not allow the wheel to be printed in colour.) Magenta represents the emergent stage. The remaining colours match those of the original series, with red, yellow, dark blue, and green, representing the levels within early

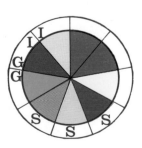

89

stage, and orange, light blue, purple and dark yellow representing the levels within fluency stage. The placement of S, G, and I, shows where, in a given level, the book is placed for its reading difficulty. The example below refers to *Fasi Sings and Fasi's Fish*. The colour wheel indicates that the book can be used at the *end* of the yellow level with the shared book approach, at the green level for guided reading, or at the *end* of the orange level for independent reading.

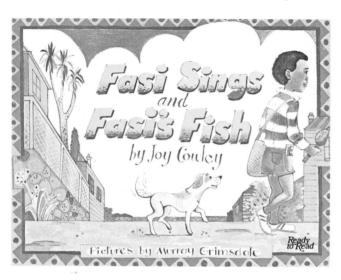

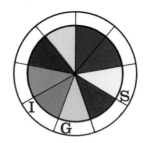

The *Ready to Read* Wall Chart

The chart gives an overview of the *Ready to Read* series and lists the books by stage, level, and approach. It also offers guidance on the sequence of the texts. It indicates, in bold type, the stage and approach where it is expected each text will be mainly used and, in ordinary type, the other stages and approaches where the same text also can be used.

Teachers' Editions

Teachers' editions of at least one book at each stage include a description of appropriate reading behaviour and offer suggestions for using the book under the following headings: "Setting the Scene", "Guiding Children Through the Text", and "Following On". The examples in Chapter 6 will provide further suggestions.

Books at the Emergent Stage

The books for sharing at the emergent stage are intended to provide opportunities for children to enjoy literature before they are able to read it for themselves. The clarity of text and illustration help the chil-

dren to understand that books have special conventions which enable the reader to interpret the author's message. The illustrations precede the text, encouraging children to predict what is going to happen and what the text might say. The rhythmical language and repetitive structures encourage joining in, and provide support as children increase their participation until they are able to read the story for themselves.

Once the children have had opportunity to enjoy a wide variety of books in this way and once they show a desire to read the text as well as the pictures, they should be introduced to the books suitable for guided reading. The emphasis on story-line and books as books, even at this stage, helps beginning readers work towards making sense of what they read, rather than concentrating on words.

Right from the start, children need to be aware that meaning is what matters and that what they bring to the text helps to recreate it.

Textual challenges are spread throughout each book and are minimised by repetitive structures, consistent sentence length, simple vocabulary, and clear illustrations portraying and preceding the new idea in the text. Initially, these challenges occur at the end of a sentence, but the position gradually moves to the beginning, and the beginning and ending of sentences. Books at the end of the emergent stage contain alternating structures, and new ones are introduced within a book.

At this stage, textual challenges are supported by consistent placement of text, first in one line and, in increasing difficulty, in two or three lines of text. An exception to this is *Going to the Beach* (see page 104).

Story content generally focuses on one incident with one or two characters, but the structure of the story and the language patterns provide opportunities for extension and innovation.

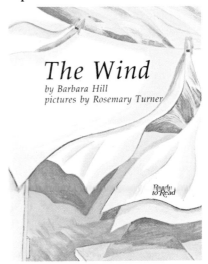

Emergent stage books emphasise simple plot, clear illustration, and rhythm and repetition in the text.

At the emergent stage, textual challenges are spread and new ones introduced gradually.

Books at the Early Stage

Books at the early stage draw on wider world experiences and understandings as, for example, in *Paul*, the story of a physically disabled boy playing with school friends. They also draw on cultural diversity such as that presented in *Fasi Sings and Fasi's Fish.*

The books acknowledge and extend the children's increasing vocabulary and mastery of more complex and varied language structures, as in this example from *Blackbird's Nest*:

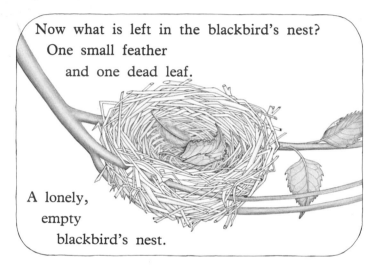

Now what is left in the blackbird's nest?
One small feather
    and one dead leaf.

A lonely,
    empty
        blackbird's nest.

The books encourage the children to make use of a wider variety of cues to search for, check, and maintain meaning, for example, in this passage from *Saturday Morning*:

> # "We helped Mum clean the car, and Mum cleaned us!"

At the early stage, books encourage children to make use of a wider variety of cues to search for, check, and maintain meaning.

Here the children may use visual cues to move from "clean" to "cleaned". They may use grapho-phonic cues to compare known with unknown words to check a guess. For example, "he" and "here" (known words) start with the same letter and sound as the unknown word guessed as "helped". "Helped" makes sense, and the children remember that that is exactly what happened earlier in the story.

The illustrations in books at the early stage do not always reflect the whole text, and this also encourages children to pay closer attention to print details. For example, in *Nick's Glasses*, the illustrations on pages 3

and 4 match the text, but on page 5 the illustration shows Nick looking under the table while the text reads:

> "Have you looked on the table?" said Jane.

Children will probably need to use both illustrations and grapho-phonic cues in order to read the text accurately.

Opportunities to retain or regain meaning through rerunning or reading on are provided by increased sentence length, the amount of text per page, and by paragraphing. Further challenges for the reader, and occasions for the teacher to set purposes for reading (often silent), are provided by:

- The variety and type of story, and the introduction of non-fiction in story form (*Paul, Blackbird's Nest*).
- The increased number of characters in some books (*Nick's Glasses*).
- The use of direct speech (*Nick's Glasses, Rosie at the Zoo*).
- Stories reflecting a longer time-scale (*Blackbird's Nest*).
- The introduction of two titles within the same book, paving the way for later miscellanies (*Fasi Sings and Fasi's Fish*).

Books at the Fluency Stage

Many things are reflected in the miscellanies and single titles designed primarily for guided and independent reading at the fluency stage. These include the reader's experiences in the home, school, and community, communication with people from a variety of circumstances and cultures, and knowledge already gained from books and television. Stories from other places and other times, more non-fiction material, and the introduction of plays, poems, games, and pictures for discussion provide challenges in content, format, and style. Some of the miscellanies contain retellings of known traditional stories, stories by the same author, illustrations by the same illustrator, stories and articles with a similar theme, stories and illustrations of differing styles: these all help to extend the children's understanding and enjoyment of reading and provide motivation for wider reading.

At the fluency stage, content, format, and style are increasingly complex.

Giant Soup

CONTENTS

Ready to Read

School Publications Branch
Department of Education Wellington 1984

Children working with the easier books of this stage will probably need to give closer attention to illustrations and grapho-phonic cues than those working at the later levels, when attention to details of print should be much less necessary. This is reflected in the range and repetition of vocabulary, the placement of words with common semantic, phonetic, or structural elements, the type, size, amount of text and space on a page, and paragraphing.

The children's ability to maintain meaning through longer and more complex structures is helped by the use of a different type-face, as in "The Enormous Turnip" in *Horrakapotchkin!* This is also achieved by variation in layout, as in *Paru has a Bath* (page 4) and "The Big Bed" (page 42) in the second miscellany.

At this stage, the children are introduced to a wider variety of writing styles, and to stories where more detailed descriptions are conveyed through the text rather than through the illustrations. This is developed by the introduction of indirect as well as direct speech, more complex language structures, the increased use of adjectives and adverbs, and by several incidents within a story over a protracted time span. *The Great Grumbler and the Wonder Tree,* suitable for use at the end of the fluency stage, presents examples of each of these challenges.

The miscellanies present new challenges for children in using a table of contents, coping with the wider range of items, styles, and emotional content in one book, comparing items or illustrations similar in style, or by the same author or illustrator, and in making more sophisticated inferences from both illustrations and text.

Books for Sharing at All Stages

Books designated on the colour wheel as suitable for sharing at all stages have been selected for their special literary quality and richness. Their use parallels story-time at home, especially the bedtime story, where books are primarily enjoyed. Children are not required to attend to all of the details of print, but some learning of print conventions is absorbed, and they gain considerably from the experience in other ways as well. They are encouraged to take as much from the story as they are able. These books are designed to highlight the pleasure and security of being read to while, at the same time, having one's curiosity aroused and imagination extended.

The series of crocodile stories allows children to meet the same character in different situations and to consider several stories by the same author.

The diversity of writing styles, illustrations, and typography at this level provides a basis for criticism and comparison.

Books for sharing at all stages have special literary quality.

94

Bilingual Texts

Maori and English scripts are presented as separate texts. This format allows children to read either text as a whole on its own, to read parts of the text in either or both versions, or to use one text as a check for meaning while reading the other.

Where's the taniwha?
He's in the cave.

Kei hea te taniwha?
Kei roto i te ana.

Enlarged Texts

(a) Nursery rhyme cards

The enlarged text cards provide opportunities for listening to the sound and rhythm of language, joining in, responding in enjoyable, non-threatening situations, repeating familiar traditional rhymes, and developing memory for text.

Teachers may use them to develop an understanding of directionality, one-to-one matching, and the conventions and predictability of print.

Easy access at eye level will enable children to use them through reading, chanting, singing, discussing, matching, checking, and viewing.

(b) Enlarged books

Enlarged books provide opportunities for group exploration of the story which has already been introduced through shared reading of the original "small" book. Once the children understand how the story works, they are able to turn their attention to the details of print. The enlarged text enables the teacher and child together to focus attention on some of the conventions of print outlined in chapter 3. The repetitive structure means that the children will soon begin to take over the reading for themselves, using letter-sound relationships as well as the illustrations to confirm their predictions. The use of the enlarged text should always be seen as a step towards each child's independent reading of the original publication.

Enlarged texts support a return to independent reading of the original.

95

Readalong Cassettes

Readalong cassettes are produced for selected single titles and stories from the miscellanies. Slow, even-paced readings assist the child to match the spoken and written word. At each new page, time is allowed on the tape for the child to scan the new illustrations and to locate the beginning of the new text. The same story is recorded on both sides of the cassette.

Readalong cassettes support independent reading skills.

Take-home Book for New Entrants

The take-home book has been designed for new entrants on their first day at school. It provides opportunities for the teacher and child to work together in an appropriate language-book experience. Teachers are encouraged to set time aside to share thoughts, feelings, and information through introducing and completing the book on each child's first day at school. Some children will want to contribute through writing as well as discussion and illustration, but others will be more hesitant, and the teacher will need to do most of the recording.

I am five.

Pamphlet for Parents—*Reading at Home and at School*

This pamphlet, designed for parents of new entrants, outlines ways in which home and school can work together to encourage and support children as they learn to read.

Each school will need to decide on the appropriate method of distribution, but the following suggestions could be considered:

- Discussion at pre-entry or post-entry meetings.
- Meeting with parents' groups at kindergartens and playcentres.
- A brief discussion with parents when a new entrant is enrolled.
- Meet-the-teacher occasions.

Classified Guide of Complementary Reading Material— *Books for Junior Classes: a Classified Guide for Teachers*

This classified guide assists teachers to find the approximate reading level of each book in relation to the *Ready to Read* series, and to become familiar with the range of books available at a particular level. The books are listed at each level according to the suggested approach. *Books for Junior Classes* will also help teachers to organise the storage of books already available within the school and to provide information when purchasing new material.

Developing Life-long Readers

This 32-page booklet by Margaret Mooney discusses in detail the beliefs which underpin the teaching of reading in junior classes. It emphasises the importance of sound teaching approaches in developing readers who will enjoy reading long after they have left school. Using examples from the *Ready to Read* series, the booklet focuses attention on attitudes, understandings, and behaviours at various stages of reading development.

The Series in Relation to Other Reading Material

The previous chapter emphasises the need for a wide variety of easy reading material, and the *Ready to Read* series is but one part of a rich, varied language and reading programme in the early years of schooling. *Books for Juniors Classes* lists suitable books according to the structure of the *Ready to Read* series (see pages 88–90). Teachers will also continue to use new material from a variety of sources.

A final word is given by Myrtle Simpson:

> . . . no reading series, however well planned, possesses a magic that will make children into independent readers. It is the teacher who must plan how she will use the books and guide and encourage children towards independence.*

The classified guide relates other material to *Ready to Read* grading.

The *Ready to Read* series is only one part of a rich and varied programme.

*Myrtle Simpson in *Suggestions for Teaching Reading in Infant Classes*. Department of Education, 1962, p. 42.

List of Titles in the *Ready to Read* Series

This list shows the titles available at the time of printing. The *Ready to Read* series is ongoing, and new titles will be added from time to time.

EMERGENT

Magenta
T Shirts*
Greedy Cat†
The Biggest Cake
    in the World
The Wind
Rain, Rain
I Can Read*

⎫
⎬ Books to be
⎪ shared with
⎪ children at
⎪ the outset of
⎪ their reading
⎭ experience.

Old Tuatara
Boots for Toots
Fun with Mo and Toots
Going to the Beach
Our Teacher, Miss Pool
Fantail, Fantail
Sam's Mask

EARLY

Red
My Bike
Where is Miss Pool?
The Smile
Greedy Cat is Hungry†
Where Are My Socks?

Yellow
Nick's Glasses
Did you say, "Fire"?
Rosie at the Zoo
The Hogboggit

Dark Blue
Saturday Morning*
Paul
Blackbird's Nest

Green
The Wild Wet Wellington Wind
Fasi Sings and Fasi's Fish
Thank You
Uncle Timi's Sleep

FLUENCY

Orange
Pita's Birthday (miscellany)
Number One†
The Big Bed (miscellany)
Matthew Likes to Read
A Cardboard Box

Blue
Horrakapotchkin! (miscellany)
Paru has a Bath
Pets

Purple
The Rescue
Giant Soup (miscellany)
Crinkum-Crankum (miscellany)
Nana's in the Plum Tree
Maui and the Sun
A Quilt for Kiri

Dark Yellow
Night is a Blanket (miscellany)
Dog Talk (miscellany)
The Great Grumbler and the
    Wonder Tree

* Denotes teachers' edition published.
† Denotes enlarged text published.

Sharing at all Stages

The Crocodile's Christmas Jandals
The Bubbling Crocodile
Shopping with a Crocodile
A Crocodile in the Library
A Crocodile in the Garden
Words
I'm the King of the Mountain†
Mrs Bubble's Baby

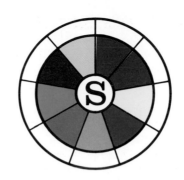

Enlarged Text Cards

Pussy Cat, Pussy Cat
Jack be nimble
Mary had a little lamb
Sing a song of sixpence
One, two, three, four, five
One, two, buckle my shoe
Two little dicky birds
Pease porridge hot
Old Mother Hubbard
Jingle bells
Baa, baa, black sheep
Wee Willie Winkie
Humpty Dumpty
Yankee Doodle
Hickory Dickory Dock

Doctor Foster
I had a little nut tree
There was a crooked man
Hey diddle diddle
Pat a cake, pat a cake
Higgledy piggledy, my fat hen

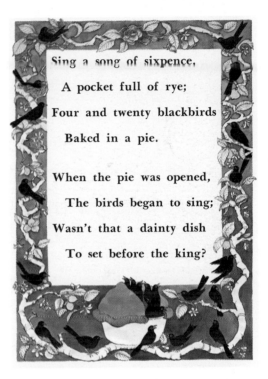

Bilingual Texts

Kei hea te Taniwha?/Where's the Taniwha?
What's the Time?/Taniwha, Taniwha

Readalong Cassettes of Selected Titles

Resources for Teachers

Reading at Home and at School—pamphlet for parents
Books for Junior Classes: a Classified Guide for Teachers
Reading in Junior Classes: with Guidelines to the Revised Ready to Read *Series*—
   a handbook for teachers
Developing Life-long Readers
The *Ready to Ready* wall chart—a survey and guide for teachers

---

† Denotes enlarged text published.

6 Using the *Ready to Read* Books

Shared Reading at the Emergent Stage

The Biggest Cake in the World

Setting the Scene

The teacher could introduce the book briefly by showing the cover, and telling the children the title and the names of the author and the illustrator. The children could be encouraged to think about the biggest cake by the teacher inviting responses to questions such as:

> *How big do you think the biggest cake in the world would be?*
> *How would you make it?*
> *What would you need?*
> *Let's read 'The Biggest Cake in the World' to see how Mrs Delicious made her enormous cake.*

Guiding the Children through the Text

The first reading by the teacher should not be interrupted by too much discussion, but there could be a pause on pages 10 and 11 when the children could consider the characters' enjoyment. This would prepare the children for the format change at the end of the book and give them a chance to join in the fun there.

It is common for children at this stage to ask for the story to be read again. As they now know how the story works, they will be able to make a greater contribution to the reading in predicting, in saying the refrain, and in many other ways, but their responses should be spontaneous.

Scene-setting at the emergent stage in shared reading should be short and simple.

At the emergent stage in particular, a first reading should not be interrupted too often.

Mrs Delicious got a tractor to pull the biggest cake in the world.

Mrs Delicious got a chain-saw to cut the biggest cake in the world.

Following On

Sharing the story again, and making copies of the book available for the children to read to each other or by themselves are the most worthwhile follow-up at this stage. A readalong cassette would provide opportunities for a child to be supported during further readings. The teacher may enlarge part of the text to encourage the children to participate in these readings.

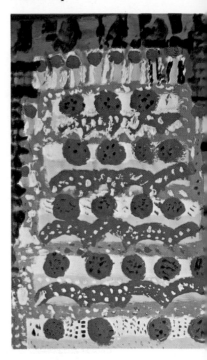

Rereading is the most useful follow up.

Opportunities for the children to reconsider and recreate the story could include discussion and recording of the children's recipe for the biggest cake, soup, stew, or pudding in the world, town, or city. The recording could take the form of a recipe, a wall story, or book illustrated by the children. The children's responses to a gourmet delight, their favourite book, or any shared experience, could be recorded in speech bubbles, as presented at the end of *The Biggest Cake in the World*.

Further suggestions for shared reading at this level are included in the teachers' edition of *T Shirts*.

Mr Greenfinger got a truck full of soil for the biggest garden in the world.

Mr Greenfinger got ten trailers full of compost for the biggest garden in the world

Guided Reading at the Emergent Stage

Old Tuatara

Setting the Scene

Before introducing a story, the teacher will need to know what background knowledge and experience the children can bring to the reading, and decide what other knowledge and experience is required so that they can manage the text. For example, before introducing *Old Tuatara* to a group of emergent readers in a guided reading lesson, the teacher

Before guided reading at the emergent stage especially, the children's background knowledge must be sought.

would consider what the children already knew about tuataras. Discussion, before the reading, could focus on the cover and include some of the following questions.

What is a tuatara? What does it look like?

What sort of animal is a tuatara?

Where does it live?

What does it do during the day?

Who or what may see the tuatara during the day?

The scene-setting will help the readers consider what is known and match it with the options raised by the text and the illustrations as they read the story. For example, if it has been established that tuataras live on islands, when the reader meets the bird on page 5, seagulls might be considered.

Guiding the Children through the Text

Questions during the reading should guide the child from the picture to the text to confirm any predictions that have been made. This will include one-to-one matching of spoken and written words. For example:

Look at the picture on page 2.

Where did the tuatara sit?

Now read the text.

Once the pattern has been established, children could be encouraged to read the text by themselves:

Read the text on page 6 with your eyes. Then tell me what the frog said when he saw the tuatara.

The reading should encourage the children to ask themselves further questions such as:

Why did the tuatara eat the fly?

What else could he eat?

Following On

Activities following the reading should always draw the reader back to the text and sometimes, though probably not often at this stage, beyond it. These activities could include:

- Rereadings—the second and subsequent readings enable the reader to further appreciate the humour, irony, and emotions portrayed in the story.
- Discussing the story and sharing feelings aroused.
- Retelling the story, using another language mode.
- Innovating, using the language patterns.
- Further reading.

Guided reading at the emergent stage offers many opportunities for prediction and one-to-one matching.

Following on, at this stage, and at all other stages, should draw the reader back to the text.

103

After reading *Old Tuatara*, a child could read or tell the story to other children. The group could use movement to share the story with others or to show how the tuatara caught the fly. They could compare the movements of characters in the story. Perhaps the children could make a picture or model of the island showing the characters in the story.

Further discussion and sharing of ideas and pictures could result in a group of children making a mural of other reptiles or hibernating animals. Another group could use the language patterns from the story to write about, say, an owl sitting in a tree.

Further suggestions for guided reading at this level are included in the teachers' edition of *I Can Read*.

Independent Reading at the Emergent Stage

Going to the Beach

Going to the Beach is another book suitable for guided reading at the emergent stage. It is also suitable for independent reading at the end of that stage and, when used in this way, its structure and content offer a special opportunity for the teacher to observe the child's ability to use picture cues, locate the text, recognise some words, recognise words repeated on the same or subsequent pages, match the spoken and written words, and retell a story in their own words.

This book offers particular opportunities to monitor independent reading.

Setting the Scene

Discussion of the cover illustration and title should help the child to predict some of the events in the story. The initial discussion could include the text and illustration on page 2. This introduction should only continue until the child begins to take over the reading confidently and willingly.

Scene-setting at this stage could include text as well as illustration.

Guiding the Child through the Text

As the child is now reading independently, the teacher should intervene only when it is obvious that the challenges are causing frustration and meaning has been lost. At this point, the teacher should provide sufficient support to guide the child back to attending to meaning through print and illustration, or read the rest of the book *with* the child.

A child finding a text too hard to read independently at this stage should not be left to flounder.

Following On

The child may choose to reread the book immediately after the initial reading or at a later time. A well organised classroom will provide options for the child to interpret the book in his or her own way and time. This interpretation may take place entirely in the child's imagination and teachers should be content to leave it there.

At this stage, children should be allowed to follow up independent reading in their own way.

Shared Reading at the Early Stage

Matthew Likes to Read

The colour wheel on the back cover of *Matthew Likes to Read* indicates that it is suitable for shared reading at the green level.*

Setting the Scene

Matthew Likes to Read creates interest in print other than that presented

---

*Examples for using this book for guided reading at the orange level are provided on page 111.

in books, and draws on experiences from the wider world. The children could be introduced to this idea by drawing attention to the road sign on the front cover. Once the title has been located, the children could be asked to suggest things that Matthew might like to read. This discussion could continue, using the inside front cover to help the children think of reading as something other than words in books. This book, like some others at this level, provides an opportunity to explore more deeply the message on the covers.

Guiding the Children through the Text

During the reading, pick up the initial discussion on words appearing in places other than books. For example, before turning to page 8, the teacher could ask:

> *Matthew has read the signs outside the shop, the newspaper, the road signs, and the directions on the soup packet. What else could he read?*

or: *What things has Matthew read?*

> *What else could he read?*

Before reading the text on page 10, develop the children's ability to make inferences from the pictures by asking them to describe the look on Mum's face, and to offer possible reasons for her dismay.

Following On

Subsequent reading by or with the teacher will enable the children to become familiar with the events and structure of the story and to assume greater responsibility for reading the story independently.

The following activities were suggested by teachers who participated in the evaluation of the black-and-white trial publication of this book at this stage, and at the fluency stage for guided reading:

- Reading signs at school, on the way to school, at the nearest shopping centre.
- Making cardboard signs.
- Collecting labels, signs, tickets (road, air, bus, entertainment), patterns.
- Following instructions to make cordial, soup, instant pudding.
- Following instructions for a game.
- Following instructions to plant seeds.
- Writing your own instructions for a soup packet.
- Writing your own instructions for a game.
- Writing shopping lists, e.g., for a giant, a dinosaur, an astronaut, a baby.
- Setting up a class supermarket.
- Collecting and reading favourite recipes.

Shared reading at the early stage can extend the child's ability to understand the message on the covers.

Shared reading at the early stage makes greater use of children's ability to infer.

Following on at the early stage often takes children beyond the text as well as back to it.

- Finding out more about newspapers.
- Collecting trade logos and trademarks.
- Making bumper stickers for children's bikes.
- Making graphs, books, posters, reviews of what children like to read.
- Discussing favourite magazines.
- Discussing other types of reading/communication (e.g., people's faces).
- Making posters for class and school activities.

All of these activities reflect events, ideas, and feelings presented in the story and encourage further thought and reading.

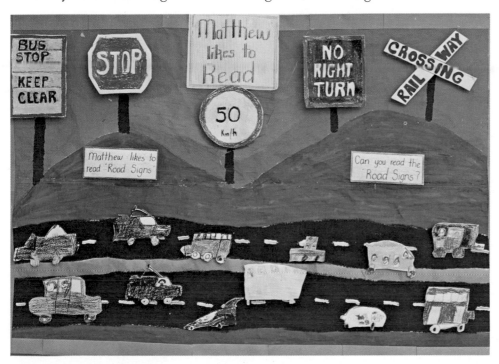

Guided Reading at the Early Stage

Blackbird's Nest

Setting the Scene

The book could be introduced through questions focusing on the cover and title page to encourage predicting events over a longer span of time. This is now possible because of the children's wider experience of the world and of books. For example:

> *Look at the picture on the cover. What do you think the book is going to be about?*
>
> *Look at the title. What does it say about the bird's nest.*
>
> *Look at the inside front cover. Where does the blackbird make its nest?*
>
> *What does a blackbird look like?*

Guided reading at the early stage makes greater use of the covers in prediction.

107

The title page shows a black bird and a brown bird. Why? Can you see any other differences?

Think about the title again. Why did the blackbirds make a nest?

Guiding the Children through the Text

Questions asked during the reading should help the children to gain and to maintain meaning through focusing more closely on particular details of the text and the illustrations. For example:

Look at the eggs in the nest on page 2.

How many eggs are there?

What do they look like?

Look at the text. Find the word that tells you what the eggs look like. Was your guess right? How do you know?

The same procedure could be followed when reading pages 4–7. Page 7 presents an extra challenge in the last line, but the illustration, and "grew" in the previous line, will assist children to meet this difficulty.

Before reading the text on page 8, the children could discuss what happens to the nest when the birds have flown away, and how they (the children) feel when they have been left by themselves.

This book is a good example of the more formal and rhythmical patterns of book language.

Following On

The reading and subsequent rereadings may be the main activity, but the following photographs show examples of children's work motivated by this story.

Further suggestions appropriate for children reading at the early stage are illustrated in the teachers' edition of *Saturday Morning*.

Closed questions in guided reading at the early stage focus attention on the text.

108

Independent Reading at the Early Stage

Sam's Mask

The colour wheel on the back cover of *Sam's Mask* indicates that it is suitable for independent reading at the end of the red level or at the beginning of the yellow level.

Before the book is introduced, the teacher should ensure that materials are available in case the reader wishes to use the book as a guide for making a mask similar to Sam's.

Setting the Scene

The illustration on the cover could be used to help the child think about the possible unfolding of the story. There is greater opportunity now for the child to risk predictions and to confirm them by attending to detail.

> *What is Sam wearing?*
> *Why?*
> *Who made the mask? How?*
> *Would you like to read the book to see if you were right?*

Open-ended questions in independent reading at the early stage encourage greater prediction, which can also be confirmed independently.

Guiding the Child through the Text

Observation of the child's independent reading of the text will enable the teacher to consider the child's interest in that particular book, the child's ability to cope with the changes in structure, the strategies employed in gaining meaning, and the child's confidence and competence in some book and print conventions. As one of the main purposes of independent reading at this stage is to increase fluency in reading easy books with enjoyment, the reading should not be interrupted unless it is obvious that meaning has been lost, and the child appeals for help.

Independent reading at the early stage gives teachers the chance to monitor how well children integrate strategies.

Following On

Trials with the book have shown that many children choose to take the book to the art corner and to use the sequence outlined to help them make their own masks. This might be the first time they have realised they can turn printed directions into action. Other children have used the structure of the story to write directions for making a variety of other articles. Yet others have provided alternative endings to the story.

Follow-on activities at this stage are often extensions of the story in a variety of forms and media.

Shared Reading at the Fluency Stage

*Maui and the Sun**

Many of the stories designated as suitable for sharing at the fluency stage encourage consideration of style, relationships, stories from other places and other times, and other perspectives of literature. *Maui and the Sun* enables the children to become aware of the origin and nature of myths and legends of New Zealand. Discussion prior to and following the reading could emphasise that such stories are born of oral tradition, that they have been used to explain origins, to explain natural phenomena, and to highlight human relationships.

Stories for shared reading at the fluency stage introduce notions of style in relation to content.

Setting the Scene

Discussion of the cover illustration and the fact that the story is a retelling could be used to introduce the children to legends, and to this one in particular. The illustration will make the children aware of a battle, and they could be asked to predict the cause and winner of the contest. Opening out the cover could lead to ideas of speed—an inherent part of the legend.

At this stage, children can begin to appreciate the difference between types of illustration.

Guiding the Children through the Text

The reading should reflect the pace of the story and should not be interrupted by too much discussion. The illustrations portray action and strength, and the children should be given time to consider these and the rich book language.

Following On

Further consideration could be given to the style of the illustrations and their significance in this story. Other forms and styles of Maori art could be viewed and discussed. The children could visit the library to find other legends about Maui, and legends of other traditional characters. The miscellanies at the dark blue, purple, and dark yellow levels include other traditional stories and legends. The teacher may choose to share

At the fluency stage, the child can begin to consider the content and nature of traditional stories.

---

*The Maori version, *Ko Māui me te Rā,* is included in the *He Purapura* series, published by the Department of Education, Wellington.

a selection of these with the children. Note that the structure of legends varies from culture to culture—European tradition favours happy endings, groups of three, the resolution of problems. Other cultures see the world differently.

The children should be given opportunities to express their feelings about and their reactions to the story through a variety of creative activities. For example:

- Dramatising the story.
- Identifying with one of the characters through creative drama.
- Creating music to portray the action of the brothers pulling the sun, or Maui beating the sun.
- Exploring patterns through various art media.
- Retelling the story in another form—a play or a poem.
- Retelling the story from the point of view of one of the characters.

Guided Reading at the Fluency Stage

Matthew Likes to Read

Setting the Scene

When *Matthew Likes to Read* is used for guided reading at the orange level, it requires, as well as engenders, discussion throughout the reading. This story provides intrinsic incentives to read both the pictures and the text and, as such, is a good example of a book which enables a teacher to set specific purposes for reading.

Guided reading at the fluency stage offers greater opportunities to set specific purposes for reading.

111

During the introduction, the children could discuss what they like to read, and consider what Matthew might like to read. The book title is presented as a road sign and this will invite discussion about environmental reading. The inside cover provides further introductory discussion.

Teachers should note that lists, not supported by an extended context, occur in this book.

Guiding the Children through the Text

One of the purposes of guided reading at this stage is to set closed questions whose answers can be found in the text. For example:

> *Look at the picture on page 2. Find the name and address of the shop.*
>
> *What headlines can you see in* The Evening Post? *Read the text on page 3—Will Matthew need to take a raincoat to school tomorrow? Find the words that tell us why or why not.*

When discussing the road signs on pages 4 and 5, ask the children to find the word in the text which matches the sign telling how far to Wellington.

> *What other short ways of writing things can you see in the illustrations?*
> *Read the text on page 7. How many people can eat the mushroom soup?*
> *Read the text on page 8. Where is Matthew now and where is he going?*

Because of the abundant detail of the pictures, and the opportunities they offer in silent reading to find particular text, teachers should not demand too much too soon in response to open-ended questions such as, "Would you have changed the shopping list?" or, "What do you like to eat best?"

Following On

The children should have access to the book for further readings. A list of suitable activities was given earlier in this chapter (see pages 106–7).

Independent Reading at the Fluency Stage

Nana's in the Plum Tree

Setting the Scene

The following questions provide suggestions for introducing *Nana's in the Plum Tree* for independent reading at the end of the dark yellow level. Note that most of the following questions are much more open-ended, and are designed at this stage to start the children thinking.

> *What is the title of the book?*
> *Who is the author?*

Closed questions in guided reading at the fluency stage enable the teacher to check the child's ability to attend to print details.

Hamish made a Packet Person.

Rereading at this stage can lead to other related books.

Open-ended questions in independent reading at the fluency stage should take the children beyond the text.

Look at the outside cover. Why was Nana in the plum tree?

Do you know how beekeepers catch bees? Do they get stung?

Who was watching?

How do you think Hine felt about her grandmother climbing up into the plum tree?

Read the book to find out if Nana did get the bees into the box.

What do you think she might do with them then?

Do you think you will find the answer to this in the book?

Guiding the Children through the Text

At this stage, the children are expected to read on their own.

Following On

Children reading independently at this stage should be able to initiate appropriate activities to follow the reading. One of these might be a discussion with the teacher. It is expected that this book would lead to some further reading about bees, although this may not take place immediately.

At this stage, children should be able to initiate follow-on activities.

Using a Miscellany

Giant Soup

This miscellany could be introduced through discussion of the cover and the inside front cover. If this is followed by consideration of the contents page, the children could find the titles relating to the illustrations on

Using a miscellany is an introduction to books of varied content and style, to the art of comparison, and to research and study skills.

the front and inside covers. They could also find another item by the author of "Monkey Talk", and the three stories by Margaret Mahy.

The items are placed in order of difficulty, but the initial discussion and sampling of contents will influence the sequence in which the children are guided through the miscellany. The teacher will select the items most appropriate for guided reading for the particular group, and which items, if any, would be suitable for independent reading.

A variety of strong emotions is portrayed in the miscellany. The children could consider why some of the characters felt and acted as shown in the text and illustrations.

Discussion prior to the reading of "Brrrm! Brrrm!" could include talking over visits children have made to the city or country, and ways in which their holiday activities were different from normal routines. Discussion after the reading could include the reasons why Aunty Annie preferred living in the city, and the things she would miss if she visited Emily's home. Comparisons between city and rural life could be continued in follow-up activities.

An opportunity to compare stories by the same author is given by "Good Knee for a Cat" and "Giant Soup". The children could decide which of the stories might be based on fact, and discuss the reasons for further comparisons. When discussing "Good Knee for a Cat", the children could compare Ann's wheelchair with the walker in *Paul* (an earlier title in the series).

"Monkey Talk" and "Flies Taste with Their Legs" present opportunities for discussing the varying use of photographs and drawings in illustrating the same type of material.

An enlarged textbook, or box of cards of other skipping or playground rhymes, could be made, following the reading of "Skipping Rhyme".

It is anticipated that "One Thursday Morning . . ." would be most suitable for a group discussion. The group may suggest captions for the photographs or each group of photographs. Later, the children may write their own stories about Leigh Coddington's morning, or they may pretend to be the traffic officers. The stories could be read by the rest of the group. Or the children may choose another occupation and draw a sequence of pictures to illustrate a morning's work.

Erin and Melissa

The baby giant wants her Daddy to give her some Giant Soup.

7
Monitoring Children's Reading Progress

Why Monitoring is Necessary

There are many combinations of factors which make up a child's ability to succeed in reading. Background experience, culture, language facility, physical development, health, patterns of attendance, excessive changes of teacher or school, different teaching styles, undue pressure from parents—all these come together, and some in unexpected ways. In one of her research studies on children's reading,* Marie Clay described some of the factors which account for reading success and failure: good readers had a range of strategies, the most important of which were those related to reading with attention focused on meaning. These "higher-level strategies" were supported where necessary with lower-level ones, such as letter-to-sound knowledge. Poor readers had few resources to fall back on, relying on memory, paying no attention to print details, disregarding obvious discrepancies between what was read and what was on the page, paying little heed to lack of meaning.

Children and their circumstances are immensely diverse.

The children having difficulty varied greatly. Some failing readers had poor language development, and so could not read what they could not easily produce as sentences; some found directionality difficult to establish (and these were not only the left-handed children); others could not hear the separation of words in the stream of speech; some paid attention only to the final sounds in words, and some could not easily match words and spaces with spoken language. Surprisingly, some articulate and confident speakers were falling behind because they "could not slow down their speech to their hand speed". Then there were those who were "reticent, rebellious, or baulky". These were children of both high and low intelligence, including those who were disheartened because they could not keep up with their group, or because they were kept back when they should have been promoted.

These were just the failing readers. When one considers the diversity of *all* children, it becomes even more apparent why teachers need to observe each child closely.

The chief reasons, then, for monitoring children's progress are to:
• Find out what each child can do.
• Enable teachers to match learning experiences to individuals or groups.
• Select the right materials.
• Organise the class programme to the best advantage.

The chief reason for monitoring is to find out where the child is.

---

*Marie Clay in *The Early Detection of Reading Difficulties.* Heinemann Educational Books, 3rd ed., 1985, p. 7 and p. 12.

117

Monitoring should be an integral part of the programme. A balanced programme provides opportunities for a teacher to monitor children's progress naturally during learning.

Monitoring should be part of the reading programme.

What to Monitor

A clear picture of what a child can *currently* do is absolutely necessary. It forms the basis for future growth and shows what needs to be learned next. Each child will have strengths and weaknesses, and individual needs.

A clear picture of what each child can do is essential.

A teacher is concerned to find out each child's:

- Reading strategies.
- Essential understandings about reading.
- Developing attitudes to reading.

What, in particular, will a teacher want to identify during reading lessons and during regular monitoring? The following need to be checked:

- How well the child uses the strategies of sampling, predicting, confirming, and self-correcting.
- The child's knowledge of how to use the available cues, and how far these are integrated.
- Whether the child insists that text makes sense.
- How well directionality and one-to-one matching are established.

Strategies and understandings.

- The child's attitudes to reading and perception of his or her own reading behaviour.

Attitudes to reading.

- Each child's interests, inside and outside school.
- The child's abilities in listening, speaking, and writing.

Interests and abilities.

- Each child's rate of learning.

Learning rate.

- Whether the approach and materials used are suitable for the child.
- Whether the child has independent access to a wide range of suitable materials.

Suitable materials.

A clear understanding of what the proficient reader can do, and of what the beginning reader is trying to do, is far more important for the teacher of reading than any set of instructional materials. Observation is the starting point for the teacher and a way of monitoring progress.*

Reading: R–7 Language Arts. Education Department of South Australia, 1982, p. 32.

When to Monitor All Children

It is recommended that children's reading progress is monitored through:
- The school entry check.
- Regular checks in the classroom programme.
- The *Diagnostic Survey** (at six).

Who Monitors the Children?

The new entrant teacher or classroom teacher makes the school entry check and the regular checks throughout the full year. The senior teacher should overview this monitoring to maintain objectivity and consistency of standards in teachers' assessments, and to keep in touch with any developments which may mean a modification in the school programme. If cumulative records reveal any children in need of special attention, the senior teacher or the teacher with special responsibility for reading should be consulted.

How to Monitor

The School Entry Check

By the end of the first month, the new entrant teacher should have gathered sufficient information about each child's abilities and interests to form the basis for future action. This information will be gained from:
- Enrolment data and the child's pre-school experience.
- Consultation with the principal, the senior teacher, and the parents.
- The take-home book for new entrants.
- Observation of the child at play in directed and undirected activities both inside and outside the classroom.

The information to be collected about each child after one month at school.

The teacher will need to find out if each child:

- Speaks English as a first or second language and, if English is a second language, the degree of fluency.
- Is confident in communicating with teacher and peers.
- Is able to respond to questions, directions, and requests.
- Can use language to express ideas and feelings, to explain, and to ask questions.

Language facility.

- Shows real interest in books and stories.
- Is eager to return again and again to favourite stories, songs, and poems.

Attitudes to reading.

---

*See *The Early Detection of Reading Difficulties* by Marie M. Clay. Heinemann Educational Books, 3rd ed., 1985.

- Takes a spontaneous delight in illustrations and can identify with the characters in a story.

Reading ability.

- Can read competently already.
- Realises that print, including labels and notices, carries a message.
- Can recognise his or her own name and other words of interest.
- Has a spontaneous interest in expressing himself or herself in writing.

The teacher will also need to take into account the child's:

General.

- Health, including sight and hearing.
- Parents' concerns and expectations.
- Physical and social development.
- View of him or herself.
- Ability to relate to other children in the classroom setting.

The information gained through this observation, along with the information gained during the child's enrolment interview, will determine the placement and programme for each child. Teachers should make similar observations of children transferred from another school.

Regular Monitoring

Informal observation is done during regular teaching.

A teacher confirms or modifies the perceptions gained of the child during the first month, and develops further insights during regular reading and language activities. This kind of diagnostic teaching often results in immediate adjustments being made, and influences longer-term planning. All this is done so that the individual child is better catered for within a group. The class programme should fit the child, and not vice versa. Don Holdaway says:

> Our best policy is to monitor actual behaviour as the child carries out the task in a meaningful situation—such as normal reading and writing within the programme—and to compare such observations with those taken *for the same child* at some previous time.*

Monitor all children once a month by means of running records.

By closely observing one or two children's behaviour each day, using running records (see pages 121–131), it is possible to ensure that all children in a class have their progress monitored about once a month. It may be necessary to study those children giving concern more often. Some children will move more slowly through the stages of development, although they may operate successfully within a stage. Most of these children do not require a different approach, but opportunity to build up more reading mileage. This gives them a confident basis for the next stage.

---

*Don Holdaway in *The Foundations of Literacy*. Ashton Scholastic, 1979, p. 168.

The Diagnostic Survey

To ensure that every child having real or potential difficulties is identified as early as possible, it is recommended that the *Diagnostic Survey*, developed by Marie Clay, be applied as each child turns six. This procedure also identifies those children who are making good progress, and provides an opportunity to evaluate the first year of teaching. Marie Clay comments on early intervention:

> The difficulties of the young child might be more easily overcome if he had practised error behaviour less often, had less to unlearn and relearn, and still had reasonable confidence in his own ability.[*]

For guidance on how to administer the *Diagnostic Survey,* see *The Early Detection of Reading Difficulties* (3rd ed.), page 17 onwards. Teachers are also referred to the *Early Reading In-Service Course (ERIC) Unit 10.*[**]

The need for a "net" at six years.

Making Use of Records

There is little value in keeping records unless there is a definite intention to make use of the information contained in them in the interests of the children. This information should be reviewed from time to time to bring to the teacher's notice the progress a child has or has not made. It should also be passed on to the child's next teacher or school so that real progress can be maintained and repetition avoided. Too often valuable information is not used in this way. A folder for each child could contain:

Each child needs a records folder.

- The school entry check.
- Running records with relevant analysis, including retelling of stories.
- Information notes on progress.
- Anecdotal records from the child and/or parents.
- Dated samples of writing.
- *The Diagnostic Survey*.

Teachers should note that information from running records and the Diagnostic Survey has a current validity for about *three weeks only*.

Running Records

Central to effective monitoring is the technique of taking running records. Because running records describe accurately *what actually occurs in the course of reading,* they provide the most helpful insights about the

Running records provide an accurate and objective description.

---

[*]Marie Clay in *The Early Detection of Reading Difficulties*. Heinemann Educational Books, 3rd ed., 1985, p. 10.
[**]*ERIC* Unit 10 is available from reading advisers.

strategies a child is using to reconstruct meaning, and about what needs to be learned next. It is recommended that a child's reading of both familiar* and unfamiliar texts be recorded. Taking records on familiar text reveals whether the difficulty level of the material the child has been using is suitable, and how well the child makes use of strategies that have been taught. Using unfamiliar texts reveals the child's willingness to take risks, and ability to use and to integrate strategies *independently*.

Recording may be done on a standardised record sheet (see the reference to Marie Clay below and the detailed example of the *Diagnostic Survey* method of recording running records at the end of this chapter), but teachers might find it useful to make records on a copy of the text, as shown in the examples in this book. (For convenience, many teachers use a tape-recorder so that they can make a permanent record at their leisure.) Keeping a file of each child's running record summaries provides a useful picture of progress over time, and forms, in conjunction with the *Diagnostic Survey,* a basis for making decisions at the age of six. Dated samples of children's own writing, both assisted and unassisted, should be included as sources of extra information. As Don Holdaway points out:

> Even after several months it is possible to reconstruct fairly accurately how each child had been functioning at an earlier stage.**

Detailed guidance in taking running records and interpreting results is given in *The Early Detection of Reading Difficulties* (3rd ed.), by Marie Clay, page 17 onwards. Refer also to *ERIC, Units 2 and 3.*

Although running record procedures described in the earlier editions of *The Early Detection of Reading Difficulties* did not specifically include the following point, it is recommended here, and described in the third (1985) edition of *The Early Detection,* that attention be given to determining how well a child is *understanding* a text by analysing miscues for over-reliance on any one type of cue or strategy, especially in relation to overall meaning—the *nature,* as well as the number, of miscues should be considered.† Opportunities to discuss the story either by retelling or oral questioning provide another way of discovering how deep a child's understanding of a text is.

Consideration of the nature, as well as the number, of miscues is essential.

---

*"Familiar text" refers to the last book completed.
**Don Holdaway in *The Foundations of Literacy.* Ashton Scholastic, 1979, p. 125.
† A way of analysing the nature of miscues is outlined in *The Early Detection of Reading Difficulties.* Heinemann, 3rd ed., 1985, pp. 21–2.

The following example shows an emergent reader (who had read *Fantail Fantail*) retelling the story.

Teacher: Would you like to tell me about the story in your own words?

Child: The fantail ate the fly. (Looks sad, sighs, and finds the picture in the book.)

Teacher: Anything else?

Child: Well, you see, the other part isn't as good 'cos that's where the fantail didn't like the food. He doesn't like cheese or pie or peas so he won't eat them. Fantails only like flies—do they?

Running Record (1)

The following running record shows miscues made by a child reading *a familiar text.*

Running Record taken on *Saturday Morning.*

"Get up, Richard!
Get up, Mark!" said Dad.
"Come and have breakfast."
It's
"I'm going to clean the car
this morning," said Mum.

"I will help you," said Helen.
"I will, too," said Mark.
Mark
Mum hosed the car.
Mark and Helen cleaned
the windows and the doors.
Mum cleaned the roof.

This is the way we clean the car,
Clean the car, clean the car;
This is the way we clean the car,
On a Saturday morning.

"Thank you for helping me,"
said Mum.
"I'm going to hose the garden now."

Mum hosed the garden.
"Please will you hose me?"
said Helen.
"Please will you hose me?"
said Mark.
Mum hosed Helen and Mark.

"Hose me, too! Hose me, too!"
barked Scamp.
Mum hosed Scamp, too.

"Mum, Helen, Mark, Richard!
Come and have lunch," said Dad.
"We will have lunch in the garden."

Running words	142
Number of errors	5
Error rate	1:28
Number of self-corrections	Nil
Accuracy rate	96%

The error rate of one miscue in twenty-eight running words could be taken to indicate that this child is experiencing little difficulty in reading *Saturday Morning*. Further consideration of the record shows that the child shows competence in the following:

- Directionality—left page before right, top to bottom, left to right, line switch.
- Using background experience.
- Using picture cues.
- Word and voice matching.
- Using conventions of print—capital letters, full stops, speech marks.
- Using letter-sound relationships, especially initial letters.

It is important for the teacher to note such positive aspects of the child's reading strengths. However, consideration of the miscues shows that in four cases meaning has been lost and no apparent effort has been made to confirm or self-correct the risk taken.

The child has not fully realised that written language, as well as spoken language, makes sense. When speaking, this child would not accept, "This you for helping me" or, "This is the want we clean the car", but does accept these forms in reading. Such a child could be assisted through shared reading and listening to stories, and perhaps hearing tape-recordings of personal reading, to improve understanding. The child would also be assisted by having stories discussed during reading and by the teacher saying, "Does that make sense?" or "Do we talk like that?" when miscues of the kind shown in this running record are made.

All miscues also indicate lack of attention to letter detail, other than the initial letter. The child may require help in developing competence in using grapho-phonic cues before attempting more difficult books.

Encouraging this child to retell the story would reveal how deep their understanding was. Questions, such as the following, would focus the child's attention on print details:

Who is going to hose the garden?
Show me the words that tell you this.

Running Record (2)

The following running record shows miscues made by a child reading
an unfamiliar text.
Running record taken on *Saturday Morning.*

"Get up, Richard!
Get up, Mark!" said Dad.
"Come and have breakfast."

"I'm going to clean the car
this morning," said Mum.

"I will help you," said Helen.
"I will, too," said Mark.

Mum hosed the car.
Mark and Helen cleaned
the windows and the doors.
Mum cleaned the roof.

This is the way we clean the car,
Clean the car, clean the car;
This is the way we clean the car,
On a Saturday morning.

"Thank you for helping me,"
said Mum.
"I'm going to hose the garden now."

Mum hosed the garden.
"Please will you hose me?"
said Helen.
"Please will you hose me?"
said Mark.

Mum hosed Helen and Mark.

"Hose me, too! Hose me, too!"
barked Scamp.
Mum hosed Scamp, too.

"Mum, Helen, Mark, Richard!
Come and have lunch," said Dad.
"We will have lunch in the garden."

127

Running words	142
Number of errors	7
Error rate	1:20
Number of self-corrections	5
Self-correction rate	1:2
Accuracy rate	95%

The running record indicates that this child shows competence in the following:

- Directionality—left page before right, top to bottom, left to right, line switch.
- Using background experience.
- Using knowledge of language.
- Using picture cues.
- Word and voice matching.
- Using conventions of print—capital letters, full stops, speech marks.
- Searching for meaning.
- Taking risks.
- Confirming risks.
- Self-correcting through reading on and rerunning.

The error rate of one miscue in every twenty running words could be taken to indicate that the second child requires support in reading the text successfully. However, the nature of the miscues and the high self-correction rate indicate that the child is displaying more ability to search for and maintain meaning on unseen material than the previous child displayed when reading a familiar text.

The second child, reading *Saturday Morning* as an unfamiliar text, would probably be able to manage more difficult texts. However, the teacher would need to watch that "sounding out" and looking for words within words were not the only type of cues employed. The child's use of this strategy may have been overemphasised by activities which focused on looking at parts of words in isolation rather than the words of a story in context, where they reflect the events, feelings, and actions portrayed. For this child, retelling the story or answering open-ended questions would serve the purpose of extending imagination rather than checking comprehension.

When analysing children's reading, teachers might ask themselves these questions:

- Is the child trying to make sense of what is being read? (semantic cues)
- Is knowledge of language patterns being used? (syntactic cues)
- Is knowledge of letters and their associated sounds being used? (graphophonic cues)
- Are confirmation and self-correction strategies being used?
- Does the child enjoy reading?

If the answer to any of these questions is "no", the teacher will need to provide appropriate assistance. Reference to the relevant pages in Chapter 3, "Developing the Strategies", and Chapter 4, "A Balanced Reading Programme", will provide guidance.

A Running Record Taken in *Diagnostic Survey* Form

SUMMARY OF RUNNING RECORD

Name: Peter Date: 27/9/83 D.of B. 6/1/78 Age: 5 yrs 8 mths

SUMMARY OF RUNNING RECORD

TEXT TITLES	RUNNING WORDS ERROR	ERROR RATE	ACCURACY	SELF-CORRECTION
1. Easy		1:	%	1:
2. Instructional		1:	%	1:
3. Hard Old Tuatara	33/8	1: 4	75 %	1: 5	(a)

Directional
Movement *directional movement and one to one matching of spoken and written word are both established*

ANALYSIS OF ERRORS Cues used and cues neglected

Easy _____

Instructional _____

Hard *language cues from meaning and/or structure are used in all substitutions; visual cues are used in both self corrections, in one substitution ($^{No}/_{Not}$), one attempt $\frac{s}{said}$* (b)

CROSS CHECKING ON CUES *and possibly in recognition of error (bird/fantail).*

Meaning is cross checked with language structure and visual cues in $\frac{Sleep}{Asleep}|SC|$ (c)
and $\frac{wasn't}{asleep}|SC|$ *and possibly in error recognition* $\frac{fantail}{bird}$ *.*

(d)

Page						E	SC	ANALYSIS ERROR	SELF CORRECT.
2.	✓R	✓	$\frac{was}{sat}$ ✓ ✓ ✓			I		ⓜ Ⓢ v	
3.	✓	✓	✓ ✓ ✓ ✓						
4.	$\frac{Sleep}{Asleep}|SC$	$\frac{thought}{said}$	✓	$\frac{bird}{fantail}|$App|T		I I	I	ⓜ s v ⓜ Ⓢ v ⓜ Ⓢ v*	m Ⓢ Ⓥ
5.	✓	$\frac{thought}{said}$	✓ ✓			I		ⓜ Ⓢ v	
6.	✓	$\frac{thought}{said}$	✓ ✓			I		ⓜ Ⓢ v	
7.	✓	$\frac{thought}{said}$	✓ ✓			I		ⓜ Ⓢ v	
8.	$\frac{No}{Not}$|App|T	wasn't|IR|SC $\frac{}{asleep}$				I I	I	ⓜ s Ⓥ ⓜ s v	m Ⓢ Ⓥ
	$\frac{s-}{said}$|App|T	✓ ✓				I		m s Ⓥ	
						8	2	9 6 2	0 2 2

✱ Peter knew he had made an error but did not know how to correct himself.

Note on analysing a running record

1. Deciding whether a text is at *easy, instructional*, or *hard* level

These levels are not necessarily inherent in the text, but are based on the percentage of errors a child makes.

    Easy—easier than instructional level; accuracy is usually above 95%.

    Instructional—the most difficult text a child can read with more
        than 90% accuracy.

    Hard—less than 90% accuracy.

After determining difficulty level, only the section for that level is completed at (a) and (b) on the running record form. For Peter's reading of *Old Tuatara*, therefore, only *hard* level is completed, as he read with 75% accuracy.

2. Analysis of errors

Cues children use when they read can come from semantics (meaning—m), syntax (language structure—s), or grapho-phonic sources (visual cues—v). Errors and self-corrections are analysed by asking the question, *What made him/her say that?* and deciding whether the child used meaning (m), language structure (s), or visual (v) cues; m, s, and v are placed in the error and self-correction columns beside each error, and the cues used are circled. This is done for *every* error and self-correction. The total number of times each cue is used is entered at the bottom of each column.

The general statement about use of cues at (b) must be based on the analysis at (d).

3. Cross-checking cues

Readers cross-check meaning, structure, and visual cues.
The general statement at (c) must be based on the analysis at (d).

For further information on analysing running records, refer to *The Early Detection of Reading Difficulties* by Marie Clay, 3rd ed., 1985, pp. 21–2.

8 Organising for Reading

Organisation–Not an End in Itself

Organising for reading has a fundamental aim—to enable children to have satisfying, rewarding, and independent experiences with language, books, and other forms of print. Whatever the setting for the reading programme—single-teacher classroom, sole-charge school, open-plan—the focus needs to be the same. Organising for reading must not become an end in itself. Too often the reading programme can become a question of juggling groups and hearing everyone read every day. This alone doesn't guarantee success. What is happening *within* the organisation is what counts—whether the children are seeing reading as a valuable activity, are receiving appropriate help and instruction, and are developing independent reading interests and abilities.

Organising for reading is fundamentally concerned with getting children and books together.

A Class Reading Programme in Action

If we were to visit, at reading time, an interesting, vital and well-organised junior classroom, whether one-class, multi-class, or open-plan, we would expect to find the following:

The Teacher
- A teacher, sensitive to the needs and interests of children, who conveys a personal enthusiasm for reading.

The Classroom Climate
- A warm, workmanlike atmosphere in which children are treated with affection and respect.
- Co-operative behaviour between older and younger children, and capable and less capable ones.

The Programme
- The chance for children to progress at their own rate and achieve success at their own level.
- Opportunities for children to gain confidence and satisfaction as they perceive their own progress and take over responsibility for their own learning.
- Children's interests being maintained because the tasks they are given are interesting and varied.

Organisation
- Children receiving an appropriate amount of the teacher's attention. (Although children with high ability might not require as much of the teacher's time as low-progress children, they still need encouragement,

assistance, monitoring, and guidance.)

- Children working individually and in large or small groups (sometimes selected by need, and sometimes formed by the children themselves).
- Children having the time and opportunity to pursue their own interests.

The Reading Environment

- A variety of ways for children to express their ideas and feelings.
- A well-appointed and well-lit book corner with plenty of new, easy-to-read books, or familiar books that have been shared with or read to the children.
- Labelling and notices in good, clear print, so that they set a high standard for children.
- Charts, experience stories, etc., placed where children can read them.
- Audio-visual gear being used capably by the children.
- Furniture arranged to facilitate many reading options, easy traffic flow, flexible storage, etc.

In a well-organised classroom, such as this, there are real benefits for the teacher, too:

Benefits for the teacher.

- The classroom is a less stressful place.
- Time is not wasted looking for belongings and equipment.
- The teacher has the time to stand aside and observe the children's reading behaviour, and to see what needs attention in the classroom environment.
- The teacher is better able to cater for individual needs.

134

Creating a Stimulating Reading Environment

As described at the beginning of chapter 4, children need a well-organised, well-stocked classroom to enable independent work to continue throughout the day for most of the class, while providing opportunities for the teacher to work intensively with groups and individuals (see overleaf).

Storage

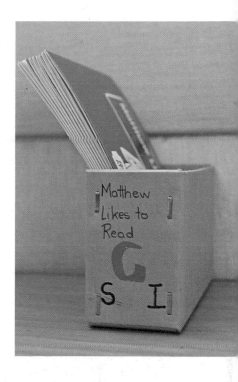

Central storage of the reading material for junior classes will need to allow for the use of the *Ready to Read* series as part of a balanced programme as well as for its use at the three stages of reading development. Schools will need to consider the main use of each book in the series, taking into account the guidance offered by chapters 5 and 6, especially page 89, and the *Ready to Read* wall chart. They will need to establish some method of labelling storage boxes. A suggested method and means of storage is illustrated on the right. The *Ready to Read* books are shelved according to the order shown on pages 98–9. *Books for Junior Classes* offers guidance for the placement of other material. Schools will adapt this suggested plan to meet their particular circumstances. However, easy access to plenty of material at any one level is important. Books for shared and guided reading can be selected from and returned to the central store. Books for independent reading can be selected as particular children or groups of children need them, and placed in colour-coded boxes in the classroom for the necessary time.

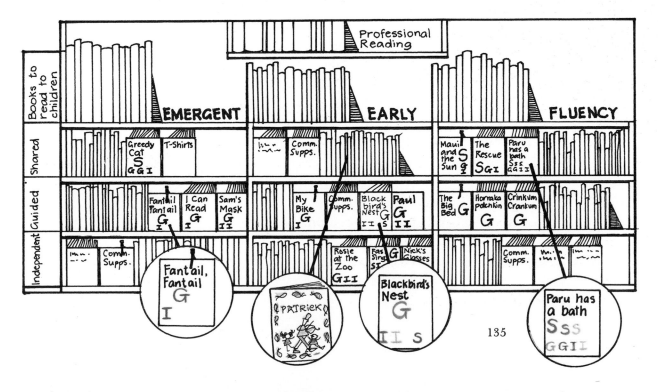

135

**A Stimulating
Reading
Environment**

A simple retrieval system needs to be established so that it is possible to see at a glance which sets of books have been removed, and where they have gone to. One example is shown below. The yellow peg refers to a particular teacher and shows who has taken the books.

The following photographs show ways of handling the storage of enlarged texts.

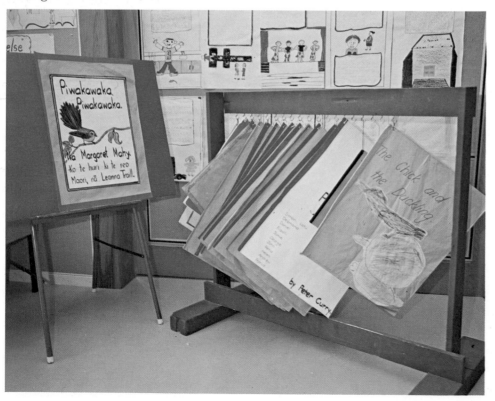

Some Ideas and Resources for Independent Reading Activities

The most useful activity to follow any kind of reading is to read more or, if children are so inclined, to read again. After children have enjoyed a story fully and reflected on it, they may wish to recreate parts or the whole of it in another language mode (see below).

Listening

- Listening to the teacher, or other children, reading.
- The listening post or tape recorder, and tapes of *Ready to Read* stories, e.g., *The Bubbling Crocodile, Greedy Cat, Where's the Taniwha?*
- The listening post with taped stories made during class shared reading time, e.g., *Are You My Mother?, Paru has a Bath.*
- Children listening on the tape recorder to themselves reading.
- Older children may visit the classroom with prepared stories to read to the children, to groups, to the whole class, or to individuals.
- Listening to directions and carrying them out.

Reading and Rereading

- *Ready to Read* nursery rhyme cards.
- Poem and song charts.
- Familiar and much-loved enlarged texts (with a pointer).
- Boxes and hampers of easy-reading books. These could include simple books that have been shared previously with the class or group. They could also include *Ready to Read* books that had not previously been used for instruction to the group but are well within the range of the children as independent reading. The difficulty level would be indicated by the colour wheel.
- OHPTs of stories.
- Stories (made by teacher and children together) that innovate on familiar language patterns,

    e.g., Brown Bear, Brown Bear,
        What did you see?
    becomes,
        Yellow Bird, Yellow Bird,
        What did you sing?, etc.

- Some simple activities involving content areas, e.g., maths or science.
- Labels on models.
- Labels and notices in more than one language.
- Pictures and photographs with appropriate captions.
- Posters and advertisements.

- Advertisements of forthcoming events, e.g., "Our school is having a flower show next Friday".
- Duty lists.
- Recipes.
- Cards of directions.
- Joke books.
- Games.
- Scrapbooks, containing children's favourite extracts, poems, stories, jokes.
- A "television corner", showing clippings of programmes, posters of actors, etc.
- A photographic book of a class trip, happenings, visitors to the room.
- Illustrating the class enlarged text or wall story.
- Children setting up a display of an author's work, e.g., books by Margaret Mahy.

- A display of personal words that have had particular appeal to the children, e.g., softball, supercalifragilisticexpialidocious, skates.
- Displays of interesting objects such as toys or children's own books, with appropriate labels.
- A display of class names and birthdays, illustrated perhaps with children's own drawings or photographs.

- A display of photographs of the teachers in the school, with their names underneath and perhaps their room number.
- Current events in the school, e.g., a display of the new book club books.

Speaking

- "Playing" at reading—children imitating the way they have heard stories read to them.
- Mime and drama of familiar stories, songs, and poems, using masks, simple puppets, and acetate figures on the OHP.
- A classroom shop or playhouse.*
- Interviewing.
- Making "radio programmes".
- Flannel board or magnetic board cut-outs for retelling stories.
- Large pictures to talk about.
- Acetate and silhouette figures on the OHP.

Writing

- Language experience stories, charts, booklets, and poems.
- Innovating on known language patterns.

- Captions and labels.
- Class letterbox.
- Diaries.
- Reports of class trips or studies.
- Class magazine.
- Simple comic strips or cartoons.

---

*See suggestions in *Suggestions for Teaching Reading in Infant Classes*, Department of Education, 1962, p. 102, and *Suggestions for Teaching English in the Primary School*, Department of Education, 1972, p. 19 ff.

- Graphs and lists of various things, e.g., books the child can read independently.
- Making and reading a "birthday book" (photographs of children who have birthdays in a particular month, with appropriate captions).
- A notice-board for children's own notices, e.g., "I have lost my green pencil sharpener. Have you seen it? Thank you. Joseph. Rm.2."
- An alphabet board.

The Book Corner

The book corner is the focus of the whole programme. New books, as well as some familiar ones, should be well displayed and easy to get at. The teacher will need to observe the use of the books to ensure that favourites are retained and that others are replaced frequently. As Myrtle Simpson says:

> . . . no matter how limited classroom space may be, it is essential to make a corner where children may sit and look at books. They should not be books that are collected haphazardly or inherited over the years, but fresh-looking, attractive books selected with care and knowledge; and the children know that they are there for them to "read" *from the first day they come to school.* If the teacher regards the book corner and the books there as something quite separate from the reading lesson, the children will adopt the same attitude, but, if during reading time she frequently gathers a group in the book corner and reads with them from an easy picture book, there will be no idea of separation in the children's minds.*

*Myrtle Simpson in *Suggestions for Teaching Reading in Infant Classes.* Department of Education, 1962, pp. 28–9.

Establishing Routines to Make the Most of a Good Environment

The most lavishly appointed classroom may turn into a shambles if routines for using it have not been established. Time taken at the beginning of a year to establish routines, foster good attitudes to reading, get to know the children, and provide a stimulating environment before moving into a structured programme is time well spent. Children also need help to develop independence in making informed choices, and in working in a concentrated way on an assigned task. This takes time, too. New independent activities work best when they are introduced into the programme gradually, so that all the children become fully familiar with the relevant material, its use, and storage.

In order to maintain effective management, teachers might need to consider some of the following ideas:

Time taken to establish routines is time well spent.

Setting Up Classroom Rules
- Having started the year in a fairly formal way, gradually establish the bounds of acceptable behaviour.
- Work out classroom rules *with* children.
- Set up a simple means of gaining the attention of the whole class.

Establishing Ways Children Gain Attention and Help
- See that children know when and how to gain your attention.
- Establish a "buddy" system or arrange for parent help, so that children know who to turn to if you are occupied with another child or group.

Reducing Noise Levels
- Make the children aware of the various voice levels, e.g., "We don't need to speak to our neighbour as loudly as we do to the whole class".
- Choose appropriate times and places for quiet and noisy activities.
- Set up an effective system for the transfer of messages and notices from classroom to classroom.
- Make judicious use only of the intercom system.
- Establish routines for answering the door, telephone, etc.

(These last three points reduce the number of interruptions both from inside and outside the classroom.)

Helping Children to Use Equipment Effectively
- Make children familiar with the use and operation of the tape recorder, OHP, etc.
- Demonstrate the use and storage of scissors, felt pens, books, etc.

143

- Show children how to move about the room from one activity to another without upsetting others' work.
- Establish respect for the equipment in the classroom and for other children's property.

In general, the teacher should do for children only those things that they cannot do for themselves. After all, they were operating as very independent children before they came to school.

Organising for Instruction

Many teachers feel that it would be much easier to work with an individual or group if they did not have to attend to the rest of the class. In some settings, such as open-plan, it is possible to draw a group aside for instruction, leaving the rest of the class under the supervision of another teacher or teachers. In most cases, however, this is not possible, and the question that worries some teachers is, "What do I do with the others?"

Working with individuals means that the rest of the class must be usefully employed.

It is well-established that "busy work", such as writing answers to questions, filling gaps in sentences, copying word-lists from the blackboard, completing workbooks and worksheets, is of limited value. Sometimes teachers feel that such work is justified if it frees them to work intensively with a small group or individual. Teachers for whom such work forms a major part of their reading programme need to look at the effect it is having on the children's attitude to reading. Such exercises often work against real progress as they give children the impression that paper and pencil exercises are what reading is all about. For example, Justin said: "I don't like reading. My hand gets tired." Justin, like many others, has lost sight of the real purpose of reading—a pleasurable, valuable communication of ideas between author and reader. The tasks he had been given had no purpose that he could see.

Some exercises work against real progress in reading.

A teacher with the dilemma of what the others should be doing while she or he is working with a group, or taking a running record, could consider providing an interesting reading-language programme based on activities such as those outlined on pages 139–142. This would ensure that the "other" children are engaged in real reading while a group or individuals are withdrawn for concentrated reading instruction.

Grouping for Reading Instruction

Teachers use a variety of groupings for reading instruction: whole class, ability groups, "needs groups", own-choice groups, and working in pairs. The type of grouping to be used is determined by the children's needs

Working in groups is necessary, beneficial, and makes individualised contact practicable.

144

and the teacher's purpose. Most frequently, teachers use groups based on ability, and find three or four groups in a class is the maximum they can handle. These groups are made up of children who are at the same stage of development and so are able to handle material of the same approximate difficulty. Teachers can suit the pace and nature of learning to the children more easily in groups such as these, taking note, for example, of those children who need help in using a particular strategy or who need to read more widely at each level. Group members can derive much benefit from learning and working together, and grouping provides opportunities to individualise instruction and monitor progress.

Flexibility of Grouping

The composition of groups needs to be carefully monitored to ensure that children are placed where there is challenge without frustration. Frequent regrouping is always necessary as some children can make very rapid progress. Flexible grouping also ensures that children do not identify themselves with the "bottom group" throughout their schooling. Low-achieving children could well have valuable contributions to make in self-chosen groups during shared reading and language experience, when they can draw on any special knowledge or background experience. The story is told of the child who said: "The teacher calls our groups 'Red', 'White' and 'Blue' now. But we *know* we're still 'Fruit', 'Vegetables', and 'Nuts'."

Children should not be stuck in "the bottom group".

Multi-Class Organisation

A classroom with more than one class level in it may present some difficulties for planning and operating any programme, whereas a class labelled "Standard One" may seem to present a much easier task. But, in the reading programme, the range of ability in a multi-class setting may not be very much greater than that in a single class. Reading instruction needs to reflect the strengths, levels of ability, and needs of the children irrespective of the class level label pinned on them.

A class label does not reveal the children's range of reading ability.

Organising the Daily Programme

To ensure balance in the daily programme, the teacher needs to provide opportunities for children to:
• Listen to stories.
• Read with others.
• Read by themselves.
    The teacher also needs to make sure she or he has time daily to:
• Work with small groups or with individuals.

- Manage the range of ability within any one class.
- Find time for slow-progress children.
- Find time for high-progress children to pursue their interests more deeply.
- Make the most of the unexpected.
- Monitor and record at least one child's progress.

A Reading Session

One teacher finds that, during a half-morning session, the following organisation (and adaptations of it) enables her to:
- Work with two instructional groups a day, informally monitoring the reading behaviour of particular children in the process.
- Give attention to individuals at the extreme range of ability.

The programme, however, is dependent on the setting up of routines, a print-saturated classroom with an abundance of easy reading material, an exciting book corner and, most of all, a class enthusiastic about reading who want to read for themselves.

4

1

2

**Class of 30
Wide Range of Ability
Three Ability Groups**

5

6

7

9

1 *Shared reading with the whole class before they split up for independent work — the teacher supervising the setting up of activities, guiding and assisting children.*

2–3 *Independent activities — painting — reading in the book corner.*

4–5 *Working intensively with one child, possibly on the book that was shared with the whole class earlier — this child then works independently.*

6–7 *Withdrawing a group of children for guided reading. Informal monitoring to see how they are operating on unseen material. These children now return to independent reading, working with tapes of the books used in shared or guided reading sessions.*

8 *The teacher now checks up on the rest of the children, discussing, encouraging, observing, monitoring, and suggesting other tasks before she alerts the class that it's time to round off what they are doing.*

9–11 *The whole class gets together to discuss their independent reading activities. There is a combined evaluation of what they were able to do in painting, writing, and reading before the reading session is wound down with a song, poem, or story.*

The above organisation can be adapted to sole-charge schools.

11

Communication with Parents

A close working relationship between the teacher and the children's parents is essential, and the closer the communication, the more each child will benefit. There are a number of avenues for communication between home and school:

Home and school need to work together.

- An "open-door" policy.
- A classroom newsletter.
- Individual notes and letters.
- Arranged interviews.
- Making specific times available for interviews and discussion.
- Involvement in visits and excursions.
- Home and school functions and working-bees.
- Newsletters outlining a unit of work or proposed trip, and/or the evaluation of such a unit.
- Books sent home for parents to read with their children.

The pamphlet, *Reading at Home and at School*, informs parents of how their child will learn to read, and how they may assist in this. It is usually distributed at or before school entry.

Parents' Involvement at School

Some schools invite parents in to participate in the classroom reading programme to:

- Read to children.
- Set up and supervise the use of audio-visual gear.
- Set up displays of books in classrooms, the library, foyers.
- Make OHPTs, poetry cards, and enlarged books.
- Help in the library with repairs, displays, and shelving.
- Play musical instruments to accompany singing.

The Role of the Senior Teacher or Teacher with Responsibility for Reading in Junior Classes

The Teacher
The senior teacher (or teacher with responsibility for reading) will need to consider her or his:

- Own knowledge and skill in the teaching of reading.
- Familiarity with children's books and current professional texts.

School Policy

The senior teacher will probably write, in consultation with other staff members, a school scheme which states policy on reading. This involves the senior teacher in:

- Seeing that instruction throughout the department is consistent, and in line with school policy.
- Organising the use of the school library.
- Monitoring.
- Record-keeping.
- Forwarding information from teacher to teacher and school to school.
- Promoting children from group to group and from class to class.
- Keeping the changes of teacher to a minimum.
- Liaising with pre-school services to ensure children's smooth transition to school.
- Setting up enrolment procedures.

The Children and the Programme

The senior teacher will also need to consider:

- The health and well-being of the children and, where necessary, call on specialist agencies, such as speech therapists, psychologists, or the health nurse.
- The provision of appropriate programmes based on the children's strengths, interests, and needs, and which take account of cultural diversity.

Parents

The senior teacher will be involved in:

- Talking *and* listening to the children's parents.
- Informing parents of how children learn to read in the school.
- Explaining to parents how they can help their children at home and support the school programme.

Monitoring

The senior teacher's responsibility in monitoring includes:

- Overseeing the teachers' regular monitoring and record-keeping.
- The Diagnostic Survey (six-year net).
- Keeping track of the composition of groups and the material the children are reading.
- Seeing whether the programme each child is receiving is a balanced one.

Staff

The senior teacher needs to oversee:

- The deployment of staff to ensure the best use of their particular strengths and experience.
- The professional training and support of staff, and the use of resource people such as advisers and inspectors.

Resources

Effective reading depends on the senior teacher's:

- Knowledge and provision of a wide variety of interesting, high quality and appropriate material.
- Utilisation of library services.
- Storage and retrieval system of books and other resources.
- Co-ordination of book-buying procedures.

The Teacher's Role

A teacher's behaviour and teaching techniques can contribute to the smooth running of the classroom. A teacher might well ask these questions:

Preparation

- Do I spend my preparation time in the most efficient way? How well do I know the books in *Ready to Read*, the class and school libraries? How well do I know the children?
- Am I providing a balanced programme in line with school policy? What have I done about planning for different reading stages, levels, and approaches? What have I done about reading resources?

Attitudes and Understandings

- Do I know about cultural diversity and make allowance for it? Have I noted how the *Ready to Read* books and other series introduce and deal with cultural diversity?
- Do I recognise that children are individuals? Do my reading groups take this into account?
- Am I consistent in my remonstrances, praise, and expectations? Do I always praise attention to meaning above all other things?
- Do I praise children who have taken small steps in the right direction, perhaps even when they show they are aware that they have gone off the track? Am I ensuring that their self-improving systems are working well?

Helping Children to Gain Independence

- Are there plenty of chances for children to take responsibilities for their own reading?
- Do I encourage risk-taking, sampling, predicting, confirming, and self-correcting strategies, at every opportunity?
- Do I try to involve the children in the evaluation of the class programme and an evaluation of their own efforts?
- Are my expectations of individual children realistic? Have I monitored the children and chosen books for them at appropriate levels?

Clear and Consistent Demands and Instructions

- Do I start from the simple and build up in demands, activities, and patterns of reading behaviour?
- Do I give clear, concise instructions on how children are to go about reading tasks, having first made sure that I have everyone's attention?
- Am I consistent in the demands I make of the children?
- Do I give children a few minutes' warning so that they can round off a task that they are working on, before I expect them to attend to something else?

Talking Too Much

- Am I the one who asks all the questions in the classroom, or do I encourage the children to ask them as well? Do I ask open-ended as well as closed questions? Do I promote children's ability to infer and think?
- Do I ensure that *all* children have an opportunity to talk?
- Do I ask children to explain their own difficulties?
- Do I refrain from repeating children's answers? Do the children wait and tune in to my "action replay" instead of listening to other children?
- Do I give the learner time to work out an answer to a problem before I either tell him or her the answer, or throw the question over to another child?

A Final Word from Myrtle Simpson

If the teacher understands the effect of repeated failure upon a child she will plan his introduction to reading so that he will not meet with failure, and her enthusiasm in sharing his success, however small, will give him the confidence necessary for the next step forward. This is the kind of understanding that is more important than details of method because it inspires the teacher to give each child the kind of help he needs.*

---

*Myrtle Simpson in *Suggestions for Teaching Reading in Infant Classes*. Department of Education, 1962, p. 36.

Selected Reading

Butler, D. and Clay, M. M. *Reading Begins at Home*. Auckland: Heinemann Educational Books, 1987.
The authors discuss ways in which parents can prepare their children for reading by capitalising on everyday experiences.

Cambourne, Brian. *The Whole Story: Natural Learning and the Acquisition of Literacy in the Classroom*. Auckland: Ashton Scholastic, 1988.
Cambourne suggests that many methods of teaching literacy are based on invalid assumptions which complicate the process of learning to read and write. He presents his own approach to teaching literacy.

Clay, M. M. *Becoming Literate: The Construction of Inner Control*. Auckland: Heinemann, 1991.
Marie Clay argues that successful readers gradually develop ways of working with print which free them to work more independently.

Clay, M. M. *Reading: The Patterning of Complex Behaviour*. Auckland: Heinemann Educational Books, 1972.
This book outlines the insights into the reading process gained through two longitudinal studies of children from school entry to the age of six.

Clay, M. M. *The Early Detection of Reading Difficulties: A Diagnostic Survey with Recovery Procedures*. Auckland: Heinemann Educational Books, 1972. (3rd ed. 1985)
The book outlines the diagnostic tests for use in the "six-year net" and describes the specialised, meticulous, and individual procedures known as "Reading Recovery".

Clay, M. M. *What Did I Write?* Auckland: Heinemann Educational Books, 1975.
A study of patterns of development in children's early writing.

Clay, M. M. *Writing Begins at Home*. Auckland: Heinemann Educational Books, 1987.
By using examples of children's writing, the author shows how children think about the signs and symbols they see around them. She also discusses ways in which parents can support and expand on children's discoveries about print.

Department of Education. *Reading: Suggestions for Teaching Reading in Primary and Secondary Schools*. Wellington: 1972.
A distillation of what may be called "mainstream" thinking on the teaching of reading, reflecting Reading Adviser Ruth Trevor's wide experience, deep concern for children, and dedication to the cause of reading improvement in New Zealand.

Dwyer, J. (ed). *A Sea of Talk*. Rozelle, New South Wales: Primary English Teaching Association (Australia), 1989.
This collection of articles by various authors focuses on talking and listening, drawing on experiences from across the primary school and from various cultural settings.

Graves, D. H. *Writing: Teachers and Children at Work*. Exeter, New Hampshire: Heinemann Educational Books, 1983.
A description of the writing process, and the implications of this for the classroom.

Heenan, J. *Writing: Process and Product. A Guide to Class and School Programmes*. Longman Paul, 1985.
A New Zealand teacher's account of his experiences in teaching children how to write.

Holdaway, D. *The Foundations of Literacy*. Sydney: Ashton Scholastic, 1979.
This book takes a close look at classroom approaches and understandings about reading acquisition.

Holdaway, D. *Stability and Change in Literacy Learning*. Exeter, New Hampshire: Heinemann Educational Books, 1984.
An excellent, short account of current issues in reading acquisition and reading teaching.

Holmes, J. *Language for Learning: Education in the Multicultural School*. Wellington: Department of Education, 1982.
Janet Holmes examines the nature of language and emphasises the need to provide for language and cultural diversity in schools.

Meek, M. *Learning to Read*. London: The Bodley Head, 1982.
Margaret Meek suggests that there is a need to inform parents about the way their children are being taught to read. What she has to tell them is valuable for parents and teachers alike.

Metge, J. and Kinloch, P. *Talking Past Each Other: Problems of Cross Cultural Communication*. Wellington: Victoria University Press, 1978.
A simply-written and thought-provoking account of some of the differences between Pakeha and Polynesian cultures.

Nalder, Shirley. *Reading*. Wellington: GP Books, 1989.
A guide to help parents understand more about the nature of reading, how reading is taught in New Zealand classrooms, and the ways in which they can help their child learn to read.

Nicholson, T. *An Anatomy of Reading*. Cammeray, New South Wales: Martin Educational, 1982.
A handy reference manual, balancing the theory of reading and instructional strategies.

Nicholson, T. *The Process of Reading*. Cammeray, New South Wales: Martin Educational, 1984.
This book presents various views of the reading process in a lively fashion and suggests practical activities for testing the theory.

Simpson, M. M. *Suggestions for Teaching Reading in Infant Classes*. Wellington: Department of Education, 1962.
The handbook for the original *Ready to Read* series, written by the editor of the books.

Smith, F. *Reading*. Cambridge: Cambridge University Press, 1978.
A concise and readable statement by a leading modern theorist.

Tizard, B. and Hughes, M. *Young Children' Learning: Talking and Thinking at Home and at School*. Fontana Paperbacks, 1984.
An immensely stimulating analysis of young children's language, and the influence on it of mothers and teachers.

Turbill, J. & Butler, A. *Towards a Reading-Writing Classroom*. Sydney, New South Wales: Primary English Teaching Association, 1984.
Demonstrates, in a readable account for teachers, how a balanced programme integrates reading and writing in the classroom.

Index

Acknowledgments

The photographs are by the following photographers:
cover and pages 2, 33, 34, 35, 39, 45, 48, 55 (upper), 58, 65, 66, 68, 69, 75, 76, 78, 88, 89, 95 (upper), 105 (left), 119, 135, 138 (upper), 138 (lower left), 139, 140, 141, 146, 147, 148, WINTON CLEAL (National Publicity Studios); page 138 (lower right), PAM COOTE; pages 36, 60, 72, 95 (lower), 142, TERRY HANN; pages 27, 84, 143, TERENCE TAYLOR; pages 11, 14, 15, 16, 17, 19, 21, 43, 44, 55, 61, 63, 70, 74, 77, 96, ANS WESTRA.

The illustrations are by the following artists:
page 60 (upper), 99, ROBYN BELTON; pages 23, 59, 90 (lower), DEIRDRE GARDINER; page 41, JOHN GRIFFITHS; page 95, MURRAY GRIMSDALE; page 49 (lower), MIRIAM MACDONALD; pages 26, 50, JILL MCDONALD; pages 32, 92 (lower), 96, 123, 124, 125, 126, 127, 136, 137, LESLEY MOYES; pages 49 (upper), 94 (lower), 101, DIANE PERHAM; pages 28, 37, NINA PRICE; page 93 (upper), SUE PRICE; page 92 (upper), JESSICA WALLACE; page 94 (upper), CLIFF WHITING.

Many schools contributed art work, which was photographed by WINTON CLEAL, ANDRZEJ NOWAKOWSKI, RICHARD REDGROVE, and RAY STODDARD.